PEN PAL

PEN PAL

Prison Letters from a Free Spirit on Slow
Death Row

TIYO ATTALLAH SALAH-EL

PREFACE BY MIKE AFRICA, JR.

OR Books
New York · London

Published by OR Books, New York and London
Visit our website at www.orbooks.com

All rights information: rights@orbooks.com

First printing 2020

Cataloging-in-Publication data is available from the Library of Congress.
A catalog record for this book is available from the British Library.

Typeset by Lapiz Digital Services.

paperback ISBN 978-1-68219-304-4 • ebook ISBN 978-1-68219-305-1

All author royalties from the sales of this book will be donated to the W.E.B. Du Bois Library at the University of Massachusetts, Amherst, where Tiyo's papers are archived.

CONTENTS

PREFACE

On August 8, 1978 my mother was 22 years old and nearly eight months pregnant with me. She stood in in the basement of our besieged home in Powelton Village, Philadelphia, trapped in a space that was filled with water and tear gas—and people. Police bullets flew everywhere.

Among those in the basement were my father Michael and Phil and Delbert Africa, members of the revolutionary MOVE Organization, who would all be falsely and immorally convicted of murdering a police officer. Philadelphia Mayor Frank Rizzo had sent hundreds of police and firemen to invade and empty our house because of MOVE's stance against injustices done to people, animals and the environment. Those injustices are still with us today.

Delbert, Minister of Confrontation for MOVE, and Phil, Minister of Defense, did their best to protect me in my mother's womb and other family members. As the police tried to drown us out with water cannons, Phil held up a sheet of plywood on his back against a broken window. He watched police bullets trace the outline of his body on the wood like a *Looney Tunes* skit. Alongside Phil, Delbert was grabbing onto whatever he could to shield our escape from the siege.

Meanwhile in another part of Pennsylvania, Tiyo Attallah Salah-El was fighting off a different type of threat from inside his prison cage. With "slow death row" before him, Tiyo was evolving and becoming a better person. Like so many of the incarcerated, his quest for a spiritual reckoning led him to seek knowledge and solace. Shortly thereafter, Tiyo met Phil and Delbert, who were sent to the same maximum-security prison, SCI-Dallas. The trio were all protectors of life, brothers who were wired to nurture the good in people and allow themselves to be nurtured by good-natured people. The three became lifelong friends.

It is amazing how the universe weaves together the lives of loved ones. It is the bond between these three brothers that has fostered this moment. The connection between them has brought us all together. Phil and Delbert were two of my heroes who I loved very much, especially because of their protection for both me and my mother. Unfortunately, I never met Tiyo, but because of his closeness to Phil and Delbert, I can't help but feel great affection for him too.

When John Africa, the founder of MOVE, was acquitted in a trial that seemed guaranteed to send him to prison for the rest of his life, the jury was reticent to free his co-defendant. They were sure John Africa was innocent, but not so sure about Alfonso [Moe] Africa, another member of MOVE. Eventually, though, they acquitted Alfonso as well and an anonymous juror gave the following reason, "*We know John Africa is innocent without question, and since Moe is with John Africa he must be innocent too because John Africa would not surround himself with guilty people.*"

Birds of the same feather tend to flock together.

When Phil passed on January 10, 2015, I lost a brother, a friend and a father figure all at the same time. Tiyo passed on June 8, 2018. Delbert was the only one of the three to make it out of prison. Five months after he was freed, he passed too. Wherever they are, I like to think that they will always find a way to be together with the people they love. My connection to the pen pals in this book only reinforces that belief.

Mike Africa, Jr.
mikeafricajr.com

INTRODUCTION

During the past twenty-eight years of incarceration I've learned the value of differentiating between reacting and responding to the pain of prisons. I've had to learn how to handle myself under all kinds of stressful conditions. In my view, the issue of self-control is central to coping with the problems and pain of prisons. I've captured something positive about the human spirit's ability to come to grips with what is most difficult in life and to find within it room to grow in strength and wisdom.

— Tiyo Attallah Salah-El, May 14, 2004

The letters that make up this book were written by Tiyo Attallah Salah-El, a beloved activist and scholar who died while still behind bars in 2018. He had served 43 years of a life sentence in a prison system he detested but, through a mixture of intelligence, strength, and irrepressible *joie de vivre*, somehow managed to transcend.

While incarcerated in the State Correctional Institute (SCI) at Dallas in Pennsylvania, Tiyo earned both an undergraduate and graduate degree (in African American history and political science, respectively); because of its work in criminal justice reform, Tiyo engaged with the Religious Society of Friends, eventually becoming a member (even though he had converted to Islam years before), and hosting its meetings in the prison. He openly supported gay rights activism after meeting a contact at the Boston weekly *Gay Community News*, despite the dangerous pressure it invited. He organized jazz groups and performances in the prison, and founded the Coalition for the Abolition of Prisons (CAP). Perhaps his greatest satisfaction was helping fellow prisoners learn how to read and write, facilitating a forbidden prisoner-to-prisoner education system, which in turn evolved into both law classes and GED programs. All the while, Tiyo was an avid correspondent with many intellectuals, activists, journalists, and artists. Thanks to Howard Zinn, I was lucky enough to be one such correspondent.

The 92 letters here were selected from nearly 600 sent over a 14-year period. While I can't speak for Tiyo's feelings about our friendship (although his letters most certainly do), for me, our comradeship was of enormous importance, a genuinely uplifting experience. Our correspondence helped me develop insights about true character, endurance, generosity, humility, compassion, brevity, passion, and strength, for which I will be forever be grateful.

You'll see from the letters that Tiyo's words are captivating, crucial and profoundly relevant for the moment in which we currently find ourselves. They demonstrate with great force how imperative it is to hear, and digest, what the incarcerated have to teach us. Tiyo's perspective, while unique, at the same time beautifully echoes many of those with whom he was caged. They, like me, are so much better off for having known him.

Paul Alan Smith
Los Angeles
July 2020

From: howard zinn [hzinn@bu.edu]
Sent: Wednesday, February 04, 2004 11:16 AM
To: Smith, Paul Alan
Subject: pen pal

Okay, Paul, let's start with Tiyo Attalah Salah-El (why doesn't everybody take a name like Paul Alan Smith? What's wrong with these people? Why do black people refuse to use the beautiful simple names -- like Robert E. Lee, Jefferson Davis -- that their ancestors had?)

I've been corresponding with Tiyo for at least 15 years. he's a "natural lifer", meaning life sentence, no chance of parole. An amazing person. He's a musician, puts together in his prison little musical groups that play for the other prisoners. From his cell he has created an organization, Coalition for the Abolition of Prisons (CAP), with a newsletter, a board of advisers, a network of supporters. He has a fantastic, happy spirit. I managed to visit him once years ago. He came bounding out to hug me with a huge smile. So, just tell him you're a friend of mine (you've lied before) and that you'd like to correspond with him and keep up with what CAP is doing. A few times in all these years, he has asked me for money: once to buy a new saxophone because the prison authorities had ruined his old one;
once to buy a new pair of shoes.   When this happens (I doubt he will ask you for anything -- it took years of knowing me before he was willing to ask me for something) you send it by postal money order.
        Here's his address:
            Tiyo Attalah Salah-El - AY2414
                1000 Follies Rd.
                Dallas, PA 18612-0287

Roz sends love. I send....

H.

Tiyo at his desk in his cell at SCI Dallas.

2004
"A FREE SPIRIT"

February 25, 2004

Dear Mr. Paul Alan Smith,

Thank you for your letter and special thanks to you for being a good friend of Howard Zinn. Howard and I have been close friends beginning in 1982. He helped me complete my master's degree in poli sci. He is one of the most amazing men I've met during my 72 years on this good earth. He came to visit me at this prison and also wrote about me in one of his many books, viz. <u>You Can't Be Neutral on a Moving Train</u>. I love him muchly. He takes excellent care of me. I shall contact him and inform him regarding your interesting, informative and delightful letter.

I thought it best to send some materials to help with introducing myself. Should you have questions or the need for specific personal information I'll be happy to respond.

At present, I am inundated with legal actions in both state and federal courts, re: prisoners being forced to give blood to be stored in a DNA bank for future checks/investigations. I'm also trying to SAVE some men and women on death row. I am housed on what is called "slow death row", e.g. "life sentence". Two brothers of the MOVE organization are here with me, along with 72 other black, white, & Latino men. *There are over 2,000 men at this prison. I'm also trying to help "lifers" in the state of PA. (In PA "life" means just that, <u>LIFE</u>!) In the meantime, I try to relax by listening to, writing and playing music.

My friends such as Howard Zinn, Monty Neill, Bev & Wally Williams, Mecke Nagel (see enclosed materials re: these good people) send books, money for typing paper, pens, typewriter, radio, sax, keyboard, etc., but most of all, they send incessant strong love and inspiration. Without such support I would have been completely lost or dead. I invite you to contact each of the above-mentioned people.

Should my printing be a problem for your reading, let me know. I will gladly type letters to you. I would like you to return the enclosed pictures. The other materials are yours to keep.

Although I live in a 5' x 8' cage, I am a free spirit. The "state" & "criminal justice system" have often attempted seal my lips & mind. I am well aware that I may soon die in this cage. When? My view of death can be summed up in three words, "Life goes on!" I have a lot to complete in so little time. Whew! ☺

Again—thanks for taking time to write to me, and big hugs to you for being a friend of Howard Zinn. He is one hell-of-a-dude! (Plus he is smart as hell.) ☺

Greetings to your family and friends. Peace, Justice & Love,

Tiyo

P.S. I'd like to learn more about you.

*Please excuse rush of this letter. I'm trying to catch the guard coming to pick up today's mail. Stay tuned! ☺

Feb. 25th 2004   (1)

Dear Mr. Paul Alan Smith,

Thank you For your letter and special
Thanks To you For being a good Friend of
Howard Zinn. Howard And I have

Still Struggling

been close Friends beginning in 1982. He
helped me complete my Master's degree in
Poli Sci. He is one of The most Amazing
men I've met during my 72 years on This
good Earth. He came To visit me At This
Prison And Also wrote about me in one oF
his many books, viz. You Can't Be Neutral
ON A moving Train. I love him muchly.
He Takes Excellent care of me. I shall
                        (over)

Contact him and inform him regarding
your interesting/informative and
delightful letter!
I thought it best to send some materials
to help with introducing myself. Should
you have questions or the need for
specific personal information I'll be
happy to respond.

At present, I am inundated with legal
actions in both State and Federal Courts,
re: prisoners being forced to give blood
to be stored in a DNA bank for future
checks/investigations. I'm also trying to
save some men and women on death row.
I am housed on what is called "slow death
row", e.g. "LIFE sentence". Two brothers of the MOVE
organization are here with me, along
with 72 other black, white + latino men.
* There are over 2,000 men at this prison.

THE BOONDOCKS by Aaron McGruder

②

⊕ I'm Also Trying To help "liters" in The STATE OF PA., (In PA "liFe" means just That, LIFE!) IN The meantime I Try To relax by listening To, writing and playing music

My Friends such As Howard Zinn, Monty Neill, Bert Wally Williams, Mecke Nagel, (see enclosed materials Re: These Good people) send books, money for Typing paper, pens, Typewriter, Radio, Sax, Keyboard, etc. but most of all, They send incessant strong love and inspiration. Without such support I would have been completely lost or dead. I invite you To contact Each of The Above mentioned people.

(over)

(4)

Should my printing be a problem for your
Reading? Let me know. I will gladly type
letters to you. I would like you to
Return the enclosed pictures. The other
materials are yours to keep.

Altho I live in a 5' x 8' cage, I am a
Free spirit. The "State" + "Criminal justice
System" has often attempted seal my lips +
mind. I am well aware that I may soon
die in this cage. When? My view of death
can be summed up in three words, "Life goes
on!"!! I have alot to complete in so little time. whew! ☺

Again -- Thanks for taking time to write to
me, and big hugs to you for being a friend of
Howard Zinn. He is one hell-of-a-dude! (plus
he is smart as hell) ☺
        Greetings to your family and friends.
            Peace, Justice + Love,
                Tiyo
                    (P.S. I'd like to learn
                        more about you.

*Please excuse rush
of this letter. I'm trying
to catch the guard coming to
pick up today's mail. Stay tuned! ☺

TO: PAUL ALAN Smith

Tiyo AND HOWARD ZINN
↳ HE visited ME. THEN YOU
visited ME.☺
I love you guys
Tiyo

Tiyo's late friend and renowned historian Howard Zinn visits him at SCI Dallas.

May 14, 2004

Dear Paul,

Welcome home from your first vacation in years! I'm glad to learn that you are well rested, eating and sleeping better and enjoying the solitude and freedom from courtship of a female. It's good you made time for yourself and to slow down and nurture calmness and to make room for new ways of seeing old problems. After all, no one is living your life for you and no one's care for you could or should replace the care you can give to yourself.

The tardiness of my response to your letter is due to the two-day lockdown and the searching of cells by the black-uniformed SWAT guards. We were stripped searched and cuffed to the cell doors as they trashed the cells. I keep a neat, clean cage, e.g. my books, clothes, toilet articles, pictures, letters, paper, pens, tablets, etc. are organized. I am listed as a "political educated trouble maker"! They smiled and laughed as they ransacked my things. One guard attempted to bait me by asking the other guard, "What do you call a black man who has undergraduate and graduate degrees?" The other guard said, "A smart nigger!"

During the past twenty-eight years of incarceration I've learned the value of differentiating between reacting and responding to the pain of prisons. I've had to learn how to handle myself under all kinds of stressful conditions. In my view, the issue of self-control is central to coping with the problems and pain of prisons. I've captured something positive about the human spirit's ability to come to grips with what is most difficult in life and to find within it room to grow in strength and wisdom. For me, facing the full demeaning punishment of prison means finding and coming to terms with what is most in me. There is not one person on the planet who does not have his or her own version of pain, and problems. I do not mean total disaster. Rather, it means the poignant enormity of our life experience. It includes crises and disaster but also all the little things that go wrong and that add up. It reminds me that life is always in flux, that everything we think is permanent is actually only temporary and constantly changing. This includes our ideas, our opinions, our relationships, our jobs, our possessions, our creations, our bodies, everything. I refuse to allow racist guards and the corrupt criminal justice system to rob me of my self-determination and self-empowerment, or my hope and spirit. In my view, the storms of life will strengthen us as they teach us about living, growing, and healing in a world of flux and change and sometimes great pain. I've learned to see myself and the world in new ways and to work in new ways with my thoughts and feelings and perceptions, and to laugh at things a little more, including myself, as I practice finding and maintaining my balance as best I can. (See enclosed cartoons and related material.) In short, I feel more in control, even in very stressful situations that previously would have sent me spinning out of control. I am handling the entire range of life experience, including my much sought-after death by the criminal justice system, much more skillfully. The pain has not stopped but my attitude toward the pain of prison has changed a lot.

It was Howard Zinn who helped me get in touch with my own inner strength and his believing in me and not giving up on me and teaching me the tools for making such a huge transformation in my life. It has been over twenty years since I met Howard. He not only guided and inspired me and helped me earn an MA in political science, he came to this prison to visit me. We hugged, laughed and talked about many things. He wrote about our visit in one of his books, You Can't Be Neutral on a Moving Train. He worked magic on my mind! He is a very special human being and I love him very much.

Gee whiz, so far this letter has become a written catharsis for me. I guess I'm trying to convey that although it's been a rough and tough week for me, I want you to understand that in my heart of hearts there is joy as well as suffering, hope as well as despair, calm as well as agitation, and incessant love.

Enclosed is the first of my many gifts to you. It is a negative of Howard and me and my Quaker friends who guided him here. You can now see your lifelong friends, viz. Howard Zinn and Tiyo. A motley bunch of older guys if there ever was one.

I'll always stay in touch. I tend to make lifelong friendships.

Stay Tuned!

Warm hugs and much love,
Tiyo Attallah Salah-El

July 29, 2004

Yo Pablo!

Thank you for your inspiring soulful letter and the ass-kickin' notes re: my story!! You have moved me to make a confession. Why I decided to hold back on the true emotions, anger, hate, violence, the shooting of a cop, the fights, the killings I witnessed in prisons, the beatings I took from guards, the assistance I gave to prisoners who escaped, the reasons I moved out when my father left, how the killing and seeing dead bodies in Korea stayed in my mind for years and when in fights I would not feel the punches hitting my face and body, how and why people became afraid of me, how and why I became involved with the sale of guns etc. How I supplied certain doctors, lawyers, politicians with women and how I sometimes had sex with their wives. There is so much shit I experienced you may not think highly of me. You'll also learn that it was the son of my sister Hazel who set me up after I saved his life. You'll learn the way I had speak to a group of prisoners who wanted to rape a young white kid who is sentenced to "life" and is new to prison life. There is much not so nice things to tell (write) you about. Just thinking about it fucks me up. I am not at all proud of myself. I'm ashamed of my stupid crazy actions. I'm sure people will hate me with a passion and will rejoice when I'm dead. I'm amazed that I've lived this long.

My sister Bette is my lifelong champion. She has saved my life many many times. I love her very much. You'll learn how she protected me, cared for the wounds on my body, would not allow the police to kill me. She would give parties for the guys in the bands I played with—man, she is a true giant! Recently, she had a stroke and can't talk. She knows that she may soon die. I'm fucked up about that. I want to complete the book before she dies. I want her to know that at long last I've become a nice person. The type person she said I would one day become.

Let me explain why I do not use the phones. The phones are tapped! No more need be said. Nor do I accept visits. I refuse to be stripped searched going to and returning from a visit. Out of my love and respect for Bette, Monty Neill, Howard Zinn, and Bev & Wally, I accepted their visits one time only! I explained my reasons to them and all is well. They understand my position on these issues. Nor do I have money. At present I think there is $3.82 in my account. The above-mentioned folks are kind enough to send money via money order that enables me to buy toilet articles, long underwear, socks, boots, etc. and to pay when I go to "sick call". They are the ones who collectively purchased a sax for me and a typewriter, radio and TV. I'm being up front with you about everything. I want to remain your friend. It is your decision to stay or not stay the course with me.

This is truly a crazy type letter—no real structure, no paragraphs etc., just hard facts of the truth! I'm not going reread this letter. It's from my gut. Bypass the mistakes, rough printing, etc. and look for and see/find my heart and soul in these words. I'll chill until I hear from you and learn that it's okay to continue moving forward with our friendship.

Best wishes,
Tiyo

Relay my greetings and some hugs and rubs to your cats!

Tiyo with his saxophone, which he played in the jazz groups and performances he formed at SCI Dallas.

August 11, 2004

Yo Pablo Alano Smithisimo!

I just received your letter, your check and the book I sent you. This morning I wrote and mailed a letter to you. It's truly amazing yet wonderful to touch base with each other (via thoughts and letters) damn near at the same time. During the writing of my previous letter I was somewhat depressed (I'm sure you picked up on my mood). The past week I've spent hours rewriting my autobiography. To revive and cause to come back to consciousness all my wrongdoings has been difficult, extremely difficult, for me. For years I've attempted to rid myself of anger, guilt, & the pain I caused people. To bring back (mentally) all my crimes and violence and write about it continues to be a highly charged emotional experience for me. Your letter arrived at the right time. Your words were **needed** and **much appreciated**. Your friendship is very important to me. I will lay down my life for you. Enough said.

There are two reasons why I am returning the gracious gift of your check. No—hell no, it is not that I don't appreciate your kind gesture, nor am I independently wealthy. Reason #1---the rules at this prison do not allow personal checks (not even from George W. Bush!). ☺ Money to prisoners must be sent in the form of money orders. This prison does not trust checks written by family or friends of prisoners. Reason #2---lots of people "out there" ask you for money. Plus, you have been losing money regarding fundraising events. Nor did I ask you for money. Our mutually rewarding friendship is not based on how rich you are or how poor I am. Nor will I ask you to help me gain release from prison. You have given and continue to give me things that money cannot and will not ever buy.

Okay---moving right along. I'm feeling much better about writing my story and will get back on it with renewed energy, drive and determination. It won't be easy or pretty, but it will be truthful!! I promise you it will be completed! Stay tuned!

Warm hugs and much love and respect,

Tiyo

*Thank you very much for becoming my lifelong friend. I'll not ever let you down nor ever disrespect you in any way during the remaining years of my life. One day, in the years to come, I will write a song about and for you! Hang in there!

October 14, 2004

Dear Pablo,

Sorry to be tardy responding to your letter. The events of the past weeks caused me to lay down my pen, put away my typewriter and rest from my labors. Dealing with daily doses of adversity is stressful and unfortunately something I've not completely conquered. Such is just one example of the many built-in obstacles one must deal with and turn into stepping stones while incarcerated. However, with all the pressure, problems and pain I remain above ground and in the land of the living. Come to think of it, lots of people in Iraq and Darfur have died and continue dying. I'm still alive and well. Strange, eh?

This missive will cover a wide range of topics, some serious and sane, others insane and ludicrous. I just may include some flicks, cartoons and a few of my clean jokes. Okay? OKAY! I'm gonna let my thoughts flow freely in whatever sequence the thoughts come to mind as I type. HANG ON!!!!

First off, there has been a humongous change in the administration at this prison. For the first time in the history of this prison a black man is now the superintendent! "Holy Mackerel, Andy!" Beginning in 1954, this prison was and still may be to a certain degree under the control and influence of the local and state KKK. In fact, the old address of this prison was "Drawer K"! There is an interesting twist to this "shit", oops, I mean "shift", change in the story of Black man replaces White man in this tragic social-engineering soap opera. The plot thickens. Allow me to set the scene.

First a brief history. The newly appointed black superintendent was one of the first black men hired as a guard at this prison. During the past fifty years only four black men have been hired as guards. Nor are there any black counselors, tradesmen, teachers, hospital personnel, shop supervisors, barbers, kitchen staff, or mailroom workers. In short this place is almost as white as white rice. The only darkness comes from the majority of black and Latino prisoners.

Anyway, back to the black superintendent. While working here as a regular guard he also attended a local university, earned a BA and MBA, married a very nice white lady who was a guard working at SCI-Muncy, the PA state prison for women. She transfers here to be with her husband and two daughters. Hubby gets promoted to sergeant, another history-making event. The majority of redneck guards in the guard union become pissed. They do not like taking orders from a "Negro"! Ha! Black Sergeant is transferred to another prison. Soon his wife becomes seriously ill and dies while working here. Hubby gains a rapid series of promotions from sergeant to lieutenant, captain, major, deputy superintendent while at other prison. When all the old redneck klansmen retire from here, black man returns as Big Man on Campus.

Black Superintendent brings with him the son of the politician who was instrumental in getting black man appointed as superintendent. The son is promoted to deputy superintendent in order to appease a segment of hostile younger redneck guards. With both in power and able to cover each other's ass, they put into place new rules affecting both prisoners and guards. For example, prisoners young and old who do not have a high school education or a GED will have to attend school. (See enclosed green paper. Do not return it to me.) There are approximately 2,000 men here. Only eight percent have a high school education or GED. Whew! Amazing, eh? There are men who can bench press 300 or more pounds and squat big-time pro weight but cannot read or write.

Last week guys began coming to me requesting help in learning how to read and write because they are too embarrassed to sign up for basic education classes. Although I'm inundated with a shitload of work and problems it is difficult for me to refuse to help the guys. I guess I'm just a pussy when someone asks for help. Soooooooooooo crazy-ass me has begun teaching the ABCs of reading and writing, parts of speech, basic grammar, spelling, etc. The men have offered to pay me in fruit, sandwiches, milk, juices, wash my clothes, and clean this cage. I GLADLY ACCEPTED THE OFFERS! I may be simple but I ain't totally crazy as of yet. Wish me luck.

Added to the above is another crazy episode regarding a young white kid who was being harassed by a stupid older Negro guy. To briefly summarize----young kid is sentenced to 10–20 years, first time in prison, stupid Negro guy assumed young kid is gay (kid is not gay). Word is relayed to me by my crew member that kid is being set up to be raped. I send word to stupid Negro guy that I want to talk to him. We meet in a selected area. I request that he lay off the kid. I also suggest that if he is in need of sex, arrangements will be made for a gay man to accommodate him.

I gave him a choice, e.g. "no way with the kid, but all the way with a gay!" Stupid Negro becomes belligerent and loud, spits out lots of profanity (nothing I've not heard before). I then say, "If your dick can reach your asshole, go fuck yourself." I walked away. Later I talked to the kid; told him all would be okay, not to worry, to walk with and sit with me in the chow hall and walk with my crew when going out to the yard, the school or the gym. Also suggested that he not accept any so-called gifts, such as candy, cookies, or sandwiches from anyone. Two of my crew members paid a surprise visit to stupid negro guy when he least expected it. Certain rules were made clear to stupid negro guy. Weeks have passed and there is an air of peace being felt by all concerned. Young kid is doing well. Stupid negro guy is healing well. No more of a problem.

My sister Bette remains in bad shape, bedridden at home and being taken care of by her youngest daughter Odetta. Bette's older daughter died seven years ago. She became addicted to drugs and alcohol. Odetta lives there with her male partner who oftentimes physically and sexually abuses her. She lost her job as a computer programmer. Currently working as some sort of assistant manager at a fast food place near Bette's house. The guy takes care of Bette and the house when Odetta is at work. He professes to be of all things a fuckin' undertaker. The whole situation is fucked up!

Odetta has become an alcoholic and heavy smoker and who knows what else. She called this prison leaving word for me not to send letters or cards to Bette or have any of my friends contact her regarding Bette. Need I mention what effect that had on me? I'm afraid that they will soon send Bette to a nursing home, something she never wants to happen to her. If you recall in the early part of my autobiography I mentioned that Bette and my brother Ernest made sure mother and dad were not placed in a nursing home. They died at Bette's home in the same room where Bette is presently kept.

I relay this family situation and information to you because when you read chapter six of my autobiography you'll learn the specific details of not only the crime I'm accused of but more importantly that one of my family members was the paid informant who led the State and Federal Drug Enforcement Task Force to my door and gave the names of the people working for me and the weapon used in the killing. He is the son of my sister Hazel. To the best of my knowledge he was placed and is still in the Federal Witness Protection Program. Stay tuned. The plot thickens!

Moving right along. For days I was in a slump and had a tough time getting back to work on my autobiography. Then lo and behold your letter arrives and fucks me up some more. (Be cool, I'm just kidding!) It was like a breath of fresh air that I surely needed. You are indeed a letter writin' fool! WOW! I hope to one day learn to write as well as you "does"! (smile) The way you explained your trip and thoughts to your partners was on "de" money! I loved the way you gave praise regarding the razor-sharp skills and talents of Lisa Feinstein. That was very LARGE of you and a great business evaluation. You's a very smart kookie!! eek! I also loved the way you gave yourself some "props" that you so richly deserved for doing a fine job. Ain't nothing wrong with giving credit to self when it's a true fact. In a strange sort of happy way I'm learning a lot from you, I shit you not. I read, reread and reread your letters because you cheer me up and fuck with me at the same time. Oh, before I forget, I've taken on the process of reading the complete Oxford English Dictionary and Roget's Thesaurus. I read and take notes and practice spellings and definitions. I complete five to seven pages of each book then give myself a test on what I've learned. Only a nut like me would dare undertake such an insane endeavor. Maybe I'm a glutton for punishment. I shall try hard not to become addicted to gobbledygook.

You are indeed a busy, hardworking motherforyou! I am very interested in learning the outcomes of the three filmmakers you are trying to sign. I have a shitload of questions. For example, why must their producers, lawyers, sales reps and lord knows who else get on board? Why so many intermediaries? Do not the filmmakers have the final say on their work? Why do many directors feel they need to be at an agency with actors? What is the differentiation between regular agents in TV and feature agents? How long did it take you to build up one of the best director lists in the business? How did you do it? How many women are working at such a high level of management? How many male and female "Negroes" are on board, be they American or not?

No wonder you type so well. Man, I used to think I could burn up a typewriter. No more! You leave me in the dust. By the way, how about hiring me to park your cars and open doors for you? Have you ever seen those statues of black jockeys placed on the front lawns of various homes? Well, I'm willing to stand in front of your crib with a tee shirt, straw hat and jockstrap, playing the song "We Shall Overcome!" on my sax. I'm willing to do all that in order to get a freakin' job. I look forward to receiving a positive response from you concerning this serious matter. Moving right along. I ain't done yet.

And now we come to the topic that we just can't seem to get enough of, WOMEN! I attempted to be somewhat diplomatic when suggesting that the trainer would not workout. No pun intended. Ha!

Your handling of the redhead was a smart move. I hope that by the time you receive and read this letter y'all will have talked on the phone and have met face to face. If not, I'll ask her to call you from here on my cell phone. I'll hold further comments about her until I receive word from you.

I enclose pictures of two of my female friends. Stop lusting! They are lovers of jazz, good foods, good books and radical politics. Smart as hell and very down to earth. They both know each other and "we all get along"! Next time I'll explain more about them.

Okay, my 22-year-old secretary has just informed me that Martha Stewart has arrived on the cellblock and wants to meet me. Duty calls. Gotta go see the new rich babe. Will catch you soon again. Bye bye for now.

The one and only,
Tiyo

November 10, 2004 [First letter of the day]

Pablo, Pablo, Pablo, my soulful buddy!

First off, I gotta tell you, your LONG soulful toe-tappin' letter was truly a joy to receive and read. Reading your words had me feeling as if I was in pussy heaven! WOW! Hell of a groovy letter! Thank you muchly for your letter and the money to buy boots and winter under-ware. By the way I like my Sephardic name, Senhor Tiyo-Baum. Happy you didn't write Senhorita Tiyo. Come to think of it there just may be some Portuguese in my family tree. Who knows we could be somehow related! Perish the freakin' thought! (smile) I think the word Sephardic was taken from "Sepharad", a country mentioned in Obad. 20 and taken to be Spain. No doubt you know all this sort of stuff. I'm just a handsome smartass light-skin colored boy. You threw tons of shit at me. My head is still spinning from your words. However, I enjoy a good challenge and shall give it a good shot responding. Plus, I can type longer, faster and better than you! Eek!

My autobiography: Thanks for your comments. I will follow up on your solid suggestions. No problem! I enclose the news you've been patiently waiting for regarding the killing and my arrest. I'm enclosing a handwritten letter as sort of an introduction to Chapter 6. The following is some esoteric information that is not mentioned in my autobiography and is for your ears and eyes only. Bette wanted to remortgage her home to pay my legal fees. I refused to allow her to do so. My friend Tom and his wife moved to Canada. He and I have not been in contact during the past 28 years. The last that I heard about my sister Hazel was that she is in a nursing home in West Chester, PA. I have not had any contact with her since I've been in prison. Bette is my champion. She has never let me down in any way. I have slowly come to grips with the fact that she and I will never again see or speak to each other. I already miss her very much. I will carry her in my heart, mind and soul until I die. She is an amazing loving, soulful and loyal woman.

You know more about me and my criminal activities than the police and the courts. For me, the truly good in giving you all this information is the fact that I needed to get it out of my system. Don't ask me why you. God works in strange ways. I trust you in the same loving way I trust Howard Zinn. In many ways you have become my consigliere. My post-autobiography plans for the future are (a) restarting CAP and the CAP newsletter, (b) studying Spanish and completing the reading of the Concise Oxford Dictionary and Roget's Thesaurus, (c) reading lots of good books and staying in touch with friends and supporters, (d) exercising and writing music, (e) and helping as many men as possible attain a GED and getting some of them into a college program.

You wrote that you speak to some of your friends about me. I assume some of them will begin looking at you in strange ways and ask, "Have you lost your mind?" In the eyes and minds of many high-class people they wrongly assume all criminals/prisoners are scum. Very few would be willing to grant me the opportunity to speak and hopefully in some small way change their views. I'm sure your friends are nice people. I just wish people would have an open mind and engage in positive dialogue before labeling me scum. Moving on.

You asked about my reputation and if I had anything to do with the stupid Negro being roughed up. In the overall scheme of things I have a positive reputation among the troops. I'm known as the wise old head, jazz musician, easy going, not into drugs or wine, non-smoker, good organizer, who used to have short temper, can defend myself fairly well. The men in my "crew" consist of young, old, white, black and Latino men whom I helped either academically, politically, legally or musically. They have a solid understanding of my personal ethics and code of conduct. Two of the crew were with me and heard the stupid Negro spit out all that profanity. I did not give the order to rough up the Negro. The crew did not like the fact that the Negro did not show respect to an older person. I was told the Negro ran into a door and slipped down the steps. I was not around when the "accident" happened.

You also asked about my daily schedule. I get up between 4–4:30 a.m., wash up, brush my teeth, shave, squeeze some oranges to make a cup of juice, check my list of "things to do", make my bunk, clean the floor, wipe off my books, do some exercise until chow call at 7 a.m. Walk to huge mess hall where 750 prisoners eat together for about 10–15 minutes. At 7:30 a.m. another 750 prisoners enter. At 7:45 another 750 men eat. This rotation is done every day for the three daily meals. When I return from breakfast I begin working on my autobiography until 9 a.m., then go to the gym and lift weights until 10 a.m., return to this cage, wash up, write or type letters until 11:30 a.m., then go to noon meal, return to cell at 11:45 a.m., do some reading until count time (12:30 p.m.), begin teaching reading and writing at 1 p.m. until 3 p.m. Read from a book or magazine until 4 p.m., read mail (if any). Work some more on my autobiography until 4:30 p.m., stand count at 4:30 p.m. I correct papers of the guys who are learning to read and write from

4:45 p.m. until 5:30 p.m., then go to the evening meal. From 6 p.m. until 8:30 p.m. I read, write and type some more. Showers are from 8:30 p.m. until 9 p.m. lockup time. I most often go to sleep between 10–10:30 p.m. I'm in this cage most of the hours of every day. I'm on "slow death row" and don't get out and about like most of the other prisoners. I have received word that the black warden will soon give the okay to give more time out of the cells to the men on slow death row. The men would like that. Being caged for long periods of time with nothing constructive to keep the mind busy does a lot of mental and physical harm to the men. What are these men to do when locked in a cage for five, ten, twenty, thirty or more years and not able to read or write? Little wonder the men become angry or engage in self-destructive behavior.

Next, re: teaching men to read and write. I began with 28 guys, young and old, black, white and Latino. 43 are waiting to start. I asked them to select a buddy whom they feel at ease working with. I then divided the men into four teams and explained that "homework" would be required at least 3–4 hours each day and that each man has a dual role to fill, e.g. of being a student one day and a teacher the next day. I started with the alphabet, numbers, number words, sounds and regular spellings of the consonants to those of the short vowels and long vowels. I put together some basic writing exercises that will help develop spelling skills. Most importantly I told the guys to relax and have some fun learning. I explained that I too continue to learn how to read and write. When they come to this cell with their work and questions, they see me reading, writing and typing. I try to set a happy positive approach to learning and help remove the fear and embarrassment a guy may be feeling about not knowing how to read or write, especially in a prison setting.

Things are going well. In fact last week two older men came to me and told the story how for many years they became friends and enjoyed talking about their families and good times while out in the streets. They did not tell each other they could not read or write but suspected it to be true. One day Dan decided to test

Herb. He asked Herb, "What time is it?" Herb had to think quickly. He stuck out his left arm and pulled up his sleeve a bit to show his watch and said, "There it is, check it out, my watch keeps good time!" Dan almost shit himself because he was caught off guard. He knew he couldn't tell time but still did not want to admit it. So he grabbed Herb's arm, looked closely at the watch and said, "Damn sure is!" I cracked up laughing. Now they are having a lot of fun learning together and setting a good example for both the young and older guys. Oh, by the way, that young white kid is helping and is attending regular GED classes and doing excellent work. I promised him when he receives his GED, I'll help him prepare for college. I want to help as many men as I can get an education so some can get the hell out of here. No, I do not get paid for helping. I'm paid $25.00 a month to mop the shower room. That is how I'm able to buy toilet articles etc. The men give me fruit, juice, sandwiches, and scrub down this cell. I wash my own clothes. I'm presently the third oldest prisoner at this hell-hole. The two men who are older than me are not well and were placed in the hospital. All the old heads have died. I assume some people round here think I'm the next in line to die. I going to fuck up their thinking and hang round for many more years.

The new warden continues to make huge changes here. Soon there will be new items for sale in the commissary. I'll send you a copy when it is printed. Also, three (count 'em) black women have been hired as guards. Blacks are on a roll!!!!! Oh, you asked about my faithful typewriter. Well it is older than that fucked-up Royal typewriter Andy Rooney has in his office. But help is on the way. The new warden will soon allow typewriters to be bought from the outside. Yip-peeeeeeeeeee! Stay tuned. If he keeps going like he is the Klan just might shoot the "Negro"!

How could so many so-called thinking adults in America vote for Bush to do more fucking damage to the country and to the world for four more years? And people think prisoners are stupid? Fuck me again and AGAIN! I'll bet my left gonad that Colin Powell and Ms. Uncooked Rice will be outta there! I wouldn't fuck that wench with your little pee-pee! I would ask her to blow me! (smile) There will be much negative hanky-panky in "River City"! I have a gut feeling that another terrorist attack will come to America in the form of a dirty bomb at shipping ports, nuclear or chemical plants. Even a possible "inside" attack at the Congress or White House or other government buildings. The situation in Iraq continues to deteriorate. More innocent civilians, women and children being killed along with more U.S. and Allied soldiers. Those who voted for Bush have made a huge mistake! It just may come to be that the safest place in America will be in a prison!

Because you will soon be leaving the country I'm enclosing a lot of stuff in this letter. By the way, I said go to HELL, not to Thailand! Can't you follow instructions? Anyway, when my friends travel to various places in the world they send me a card or two. I ask that you do the same. Just what the fuck am I supposed to do while waiting for your narrow ass to return? It has just popped into my mind that we met via the mails during the month of February of this year. It's been nine months and I'm still trying to figure out which one of us is pregnant! Eek! That's what you get for saying "Fuck Me" too many times! I gotta tell Howard Zinn about this!

Your not-so-good experience with that TV interview was indeed fucked up with some good and bad. The bad was those shitty questions posed by Chris Cuomo. The good was the satellite feed getting lost. I'm glad you have the balls to take such risks. I'd do the same! The powers that be will never allow me to speak to the public about prisons or my life. It's up to you to get the job done.

Hey, when you informed me that your close friend is the eldest daughter of Malcolm X, you shocked the shit out of me. Man, there is nothing you can learn from me. Malcolm's family are truly giants. I'm expecting the next thing you'll let me in on is that you painted those lawn jockeys, viz. Kizzy, Uncle Tom and Aunt Jemima, WHITE!!!!!!!

Some closing thoughts. Who are your favorite jazz musicians and singers? Relay my greetings to your mom and dad. I was going to include a note to them describing how you and I met but that would be inappropriate. Maybe later on and only with your permission would I do so. Hey, still no NY Times or book as of yet. Man, my fingers are getting numb. Gotta close. I wish you an excellent vacation with plenty of rest, good food, maybe a bit of pussy. (Ha!) Have a happy eight days of Hanukkah. I'll miss your sorry ass and so will the cats. Come back safe and sane! I keep you locked in my thoughts and prayers. Take care. God bless you.

Tiyo

Yo! When you return I'll discuss the possibility of talking to you via a 5 min. phone call. Something to look forward to, eh?

I just received notice I am to meet with the new warden on November 15th. Oh shit! I hope he won't order me shot! Why me?

November 10, 2004 [Second letter of the day]

Pablo!

Enclosed are the final eight pages to chapter six that focus on the events leading up to the killing and my arrest. Writing about the crazy shit was difficult. I experienced some flashbacks that were ugly. I want to refrain from looking back and reviewing all the negative stupid crap in my life. Such type thinking depletes my energy and hinders me from concentrating on the present and moving forward with positive projects.

Therefore, I do not think it necessary to write specific details regarding my state and federal trials or to give names of hostile or supportive witnesses, nor the names of the people I did business with. The prosecution offered me a deal if I would name names. I refused. I don't have what it must take to become a snitch. I have adjusted as best I can to being a productive prisoner. I detest being incarcerated and prison per se. That is the major impetus for my work to help abolish prisons as we presently know prisons to be.

Sometimes I desire immediate victory over my past fuckups, even though common sense tells me that I've still got plenty of dues to pay. Every step in my rehabilitation comes with its own set of requirements that must be followed to get to the next step. I'm nowhere near becoming a hero or saint. I'm not in any way striving to be like those type folks. I'm trying as best I can to clean up my act during these final years of my crazy-ass life. My days of being an outlaw have long passed. I's now a rather nice "Negro"!!

I await your fastidious comments regarding my work.

Adios MotherForYou!
Tiyo

December 1, 2004

Pablo!!!!
I just received the NY Times!

Thank you very much!! Yippeeeeeeeeeeee.

The mailroom informed me that the address is not correct. Don't worry! I'll write a note to the Times re: my correct address.

Man, you don't know how happy you've made me with this gift of the NY Times. I love to read and learn new things every day! I'll share it with the guys.

Huge warm hugs of love!

Tiyo

**I forgot to inform you that the new Negro warden made some offers to me, e.g. (1) Did I want to be moved off "slow death row" near or in the hospital? I said, "Thanks, but no thanks!" I don't want to be around sick & dying prisoners. (2) He said he would ask the man in charge of the school to hire me as a "teacher's aide" since I'm already teaching and preparing guys to enter the GED program. I said I'll think about it and will let him know my decision after the holidays. Later I'll explain to you my reasons for refusing such a job, e.g. I'll have to walk a long way in the ice and snow 3 times a day to get to the school and back to this cage. (3) He said, "Tiyo you are an excellent role model and I would like you to speak to outside guests who plan to visit this prison." What do you think I should do?

Love you man!
Tiyo

Dec 30, 2004

Dear Tiyo —

Just got your letter
and phoned Paul Alan's
office. They tell me he
is okay.
Thanks for alerting
me — I had forgotten
that he would be in Thailand.
I will tell Paul
how concerned you were.

Love —

Howard

December 31, 2004

Dear Pablo,

Things here have come to a halt. All the guys are concerned about you. Not much holiday cheer going on. I put the "Read, Write, and Be Free" program on hold until I hear from you. I've asked folks on the outside to call your office and seek information about you. I hope that soon someone will contact me.

I've sent letters to your PO box and your office. I assume the people at your office are beginning to wonder who is this guy Tiyo and why is he sending all these letters to Pablo? Easy to answer that question. Pablo is my close friend and I'm worried about him. Sure do miss you.

Sincerely,
Tiyo

2005
"THE NEW BLACK WARDEN"

January 6, 2005 (Thursday 3:45 p.m.)

Hello Pablo! ☺

Approximately 10 minutes ago I received letters from Howard Zinn, Monty Neill, Bev and Wally Williams informing me that they called your office and were told "Pablo is okay!"

Howard thanked me for alerting him that you left for Thailand. He said he would call you and relay my greetings and concern. I was deeply worried. I sent letters to a lot of people informing them to call your office. Man, I could not eat or sleep. Guys came by thinking I was about to leave this planet. I lost weight. When it comes to my sister Bette, Howard & Roz, Monty & Shelley, Bev & Wally, Elizabeth Dede, and YOU, I'm a pure pussy! I usually type 4 to 5 pages to you. My hands were shaking too much to type. I did send brief notes to your office and PO box. People at your office must think I'm a crazy-ass convict for mailing all those letters to you. I'm so fucking happy to learn you are safe. Whew! I have a lot of news to relate to you but now I'm going to get ready to eat something. My narrow old bony ass "is ah hungry"! Please contact your mom, dad, sister and all your close friends. I'm sure they too were worried about you. I'm going to sleep long and hard tonight.

The 4,000-pound monster has been casted off my back!

Welcome home!

Warm hugs and much love!

Your lifelong quote "colored" friend,

Tiyo

P.S. The cats send their love. ☺

January 10th, 2005

Welcome home Pablo!

It is great to know you are safe! It also feels good to again type a letter to you. There are a lot of items on "de agenda" to relay to you. I'm going to let my thoughts flow free and natural, no specific order. Subjects may jump around a lot. Brace yourself!

The new black warden approved all the recommendations I suggested to him. A few days before Christmas a 24-inch color TV hooked up on the cable channel was placed in the day room. It stays on from 6 a.m. until 9 p.m. every day. Books, magazines, board games, ping-pong, etc. are available in the day room. Also, the doors on slow death row are now open from 6:30 a.m. until 12:30, then closed during count from 12:30 to 1 p.m., then open from 1 p.m. to 4 p.m., then closed for count at 4:30 p.m., then again opened from 6–9 p.m. Chow lines are at the same time. The guards on this cellblock have not yet got used to seeing 120 "killers" roaming around outside the cells and in the day room. The guards can no longer lock us in then go to sleep until chow time.

I was asked to organize a Christmas show. My crew relayed word to interested guys who wanted to perform. The show was held in the gym and the turnout was great. The men enjoyed playing and the guys in the audience cheered certain groups and booed other groups. I asked two gay guys and the biggest and strongest black weight lifter to MC the program. They did an excellent job and had the audience crackin' up laughing. I'm now hoping that the new warden will give approval to restart the music program. There are at least $30-40,000 worth of instruments and equipment in the band room that are not being used. The need to start music classes is important.

I was again asked if I wanted to be moved off slow death row. I refused. I've been here for 25 years. I'd rather someone else be approved to leave this cellblock. I'm okay. I'm the oldest man here and the guys take care of me.

The NY Times has become a big hit around here. After the paper is passed around and read by everyone, I then give the okay to have various sections, pictures, etc. cut out. Some guys like the pictures of new cars, others dig the entertainment section and of course the sports section. My crew members enjoy the national, international and metro sections. They have some spirited political discussions. There are two guys who dig the food and fashion sections. The paper is much appreciated by all of us.

Next the "reading and writing" project. When we first started we had 20 to 40 guys in the program. I spent the money you sent me for supplies and at Christmas I gave each man a candy bar and a bag of chips. I told them it was your gift to each man. Within a few days I received request from over a hundred men wanting to get in the program. I respectfully told them I would have to put them on the waiting list until you returned from Thailand because I do not have money for supplies to get them started. I also explained that each man who qualifies and is accepted in the regular GED school program, I will ask that he purchase at least $1.00 worth of supplies from the commissary in order to help finance the next group of men who desire to get into our program. I want to prove to the men that we can and will become self-sustaining and responsible for our own welfare. I told them that once we get up and running we can move towards studying criminal and civil law and help some of the men get into college. I want the men to learn to become self-reliant and create new ways to think, organize and accomplish positive goals. We can, in time, turn slow death row into a learning center. I told them I'm not always going to be around. My job is to help bring about new leaders and organizers. Once the men realize their own inner power they can and will surpass everything I've accomplished. They will zoom on by me and soar to new heights and push the struggle forward.

What did you do in Thailand before and after the tsunami? Do you have friends there? How is the food, drinks, art, music, etc.? Do you want to return to Thailand?

By the way, I would have loved hearing the presentation you gave to the people at your office. I have this rather happy inner feeling that our manner of speaking to large and small groups of people is somewhat similar. I also practice and time myself before giving a speech. There is a saying "failure to prepare is to prepare for failure!" I don't like to fail.

Okkkkkkkkkkkkkkkkk, enough for today. I'm going to take a piss, then rest a bit. I'm not yet up to full speed. When I'm feeling better I shall tease you till tears flow from your eyes and your tummy will ache from laughing long and hard. So stay tuned!! I'll catch you soon again.

Welcome home!!!! Warm hugs and much love,
Teeeee-Toe!

Jan 15, 2005

Dear Tiyo—

Thanks so much
for that marvelous story
about you + the Jon Stewart
show + the other guys in
the day room and the reaction
of the inmates + guards (!)
to your presentation.
It's one for the books!

Roz + I send love,

Howard

April 14, 2005

Yo Pablo,

This will be a not so bad not so good news letter about what has taken place at this prison during your trip to and from Thailand.

First off, our reading and writing project filled the school with men studying for their GEDs. Word was sent to me not to send any more students during this school term because the classrooms are full and only able to accommodate 20 students at a time in the four classrooms. There are only four classrooms for incoming GED students. The remaining three classrooms are for computer classes, English as a second language (for Hispanic prisoners), and social studies for prisoners preparing for college courses. My crew members are enrolled in the college courses and helping tutor GED students. Within the coming two years they will earn associate degrees. They are younger, stronger and a lot smarter than me and will be released in the coming four years. I am super proud of these men.

Just before you left for Thailand I ran out of supplies for the men studying on the cellblocks. The guys wanted to send a gang of thieves to steal supplies from the school library and warehouse in order to keep things moving. I did not allow that to happen because if anyone would get busted they would be placed in "the Hole" and our program would be shut down. I decided to ask each of my crew members to loan me enough money to buy the supplies from the commissary. I promised to repay them in the offing. (smile) None of us have much money but as a team we've been able to keep things moving forward in a positive manner.

Now comes the crazy news. During the past 2 months there have been 14 deaths at this prison. Two of the deaths happened on this cellblock (also known as "slow death row"). There are 115 of us housed on this cellblock. Two MOVE brothers, Phil and Del Africa, are on this cellblock. We get along very well. They help take care of me when I'm not feeling well or they will stop by to talk about jazz, art, prisons, and world events. We used to lift weights together until my age caught up with me. Now I sometimes watch them workout while I do yoga.

Anyway, the first guy died (we assume) at approximately 1 a.m. and remained in the cell until 6:30 a.m. before the change of shift when the morning guards began their count. When the morning guard reached the cell and called for the man to stand up for count the guard unlocked the cell door, went into the cell and yelled, "Holy shit, he is dead!" The second guard ran to the cell and called the hospital and "control" for help. When the hospital people arrived and carried the man out of the cell and on to the gurney rigor mortis had set in and the guy was stiff as a board. He was 67 years old, sentenced to "life", no family or outside support, worked in the mattress factory for 28 years sweeping the floor. Never went outside in the yard, did not read books, smoked a pack of cigarettes a day. Little wonder he died. He gave up trying to live.

The next guy died a week later. He was in the cell next to me. He weighed 340–350 lbs. He ate all kinds of junk food, drank sodas, did not exercise, and was a heavy smoker. He died in the cell at approximately 2:15 a.m. At about 2 a.m. he began hitting on the wall and calling my name asking for help. I called for the guard, who was asleep at the guard desk. The sound of my voice woke up a lot of the guys on the cellblock and they began calling the guard. When the guard arrived at the cell that I'm in he asked, "What's the matter?" I said, "The guy next to me is sick, check to see if he is okay!" The stupid guard looks in the cell and starts asking the guy, "Are you okay?" when in fact the guy is lying on floor dead. Finally the guard realizes the man has either passed out or is dead. The guard forgot to bring his cell phone and has to go back to the front of the cellblock to make a call to the hospital and to "control" for backup guards. When the hospital person and two other guards arrive and unlock the cell door, the hospital person checks the body and tells the guards the man is dead. That set off a rerun of the "Keystone Kops" in action. No shit! I have never before witnessed such confusion. Check this out. They did not have rubber gloves and did not want to touch the body. By pure luck I had 7 pairs of rubber gloves that were given to me by the morning guards to give to the guys who clean the cell that I'm in. I gave the gloves to the hospital worker and the guards. The cells are small and only two guards could get in the cell and step over the body to try to pick up the dead man. Remember the dead guy weighs 340–350 lbs. I assume the dead weight total is a lot more. The two guards could not pick up the body. They tried for ten min. and could not get the guy out of the cell. I suggested they roll the body on its side and place a blanket under the body and pull the body out of the cell. Finally they get the body out of the cell by pulling it out on the blanket. Now they can't get the body into the wheelchair. They call for more help. Four more guards arrive with the shift captain. All of this is taking place on the second tier which is very narrow, e.g. two-and-a-half-feet wide. The guards are bumping into each other and cussing because they can't get the body in the wheelchair. The guys on the cellblock are yelling and cussing. The cellblock is dark. Then someone turns on their radio full blast to a hard rock station and pushes the noise level up and away. There are 117 men on this cellblock wondering what the fuck is going on. The men in the front of the cellblock think it's me the guards are working on. (Stop laughing!) It took three quarters of an hour for the guards to get the body in the wheelchair. When they get to the stairs to go down to the first floor they can't control the wheelchair as they begin to go down the steps. Lo and behold the body falls out of the wheelchair. Man, the whole thing was ugly.

The following day I was called to the unit manager's office and asked for suggestions on ways that would improve the manner in which the guards could respond should other prisoners become ill and are in need of swift medical attention at night when the lights are turned off and cellblock is locked down.

I went into what I now call my "Pablo mode". It was an imitation of the presentation you gave to your colleagues at the agency. I did a solid 10–15 minute talk about the guards sleeping and not checking the cells every half hour, not having their cell phones, guards not knowing how to remove a body from a cell, and not having a wheelchair on the cellblock. I suggested the guards should be trained in CPR and men who are not well be moved downstairs and near the front of the cellblock and the shift captain should come to the cellblock at least twice during the night between 10 p.m. and 6 a.m. and check to see if the guard is awake. I told him that I hope the guards handle my body with more dignity when I die than they did the manner in which they misused the guy who was next to me. The unit manager thanked me and said he would talk to the superintendent to implement the suggestions as soon as possible. I'm pleased to report that on this past Monday new guards have been assigned to this cellblock and they are checking every half hour to see if everyone is still living, at least until the morning shift arrives. So far so good. No one has died last week or this week.

Man, I've got to go eat. It's chow time. My next letter will be a bit more pleasant, e.g. it will be about art, women, music, your travels to visit family and friends. So stay tuned. Over and out!

The one and only,
TeeeeeeeeeeeeeeOOOOOOOOOOOH!

April 27, 2005

Dear Pablo,

Thank you for your recent letter and the return of the legal brief. Good to learn you are okay and super busy. Before I respond to your concerns regarding the CAP newsletter and my autobiography allow me to give a brief summary of the events that transpired at this hell-hole during the past few weeks.

The prison was locked down. Guards from another prison dressed in black handcuffed us (hands behind our backs) and searched everyone and everywhere and every cell. They trashed our belongings and threw out sheets, pillow cases, towels, newspapers, magazines, rugs, soap, toilet paper, and fruit. They did a sweep of the entire prison, the kitchen, mattress factory, garment plant and the hospital. Twenty large dump trucks made many trips to and from the dump site hauling away tons of crap. The guards arrived at 5:30 a.m. and stayed until 6:30 p.m. We were fed in the cells. The hospital staff was rushing around giving out various medications and shots to the diabetics and taking blood pressures.

The causes for the lockdown: (1) prisoners fighting guards, (2) prisoners fighting each other, (3) prisoners cutting each other, and (4) one out of control prisoner stalking and raping a homosexual. All of these events took place on the other side of the prison, not here on slow death row. Some prisoners have been transferred. New oppressive rules are now in place. It has taken three days for me to reorganize this cage. I along with the majority of men on this cellblock are not happy campers. I have not been in my usual positive happy state of mind. Believe me prison life sucks big time!

Regarding the CAP material I sent you. I do not want you or Howard Zinn to become involved with that project. The reason I send you guys such material is to keep you posted as to my activities, plans and projects. The success or failure of my work depends entirely on me. It is my responsibility to make things succeed. I set the bar high and continue challenging myself. Hell, I don't always succeed in my endeavors. Many times I've had to confront and deal with all sorts of adversity and defeats. Still, I refuse to give up easily. For me, if it's meant to happen, it will happen. If not, I'll move on to another project. I cannot and will not sit around in this prison wasting my time as do the majority of prisoners playing cards, basketball, gazing at cartoons and soap operas in the day room, or engaging in meaningless conversations. I enjoy reading, writing, practicing and writing music, and learning things with and from my crew. Sometimes I choose to be alone. I enjoy my own company.

Now to my autobiography. Thank you muchly for discussing the situation with Howard. As I mentioned before, I don't know anything about the publishing business. It appears that publishing a book costs big bucks. If that is the case I think it best to consider possible alternatives. I would never ask you or Howard to pay the total cost for the publication of my autobiography. I think I mentioned that I plan to ask certain people to donate whatever they can afford to help pay the costs of the project. Enclosed is a list of such people. I have no plans to put the book on sale to the general public. The general public is not at all interested in my life. The story is my gift to my sister and all you good folks who helped me survive.

Therefore, let's try to locate someone and pay them to type the story on a computer in a font size that would be easy to read. Then have copies made and a regular office-type cover placed around the pages and mailed to each donor. I assume such will not cost as much as the costs of publishing a book. Yes, I too will donate money to the project. I'll start saving money right away. I hate having to beg people for $. I'd rather sell my keyboard, sax and radio. It could take 9—10 months for me to save $100. That will be the amount I'll request each person on the list to donate. I will need help in locating someone to type the story on a computer. Maybe a college student or retired person who could use some extra money. And by the way, I do not want you to be the "point man" in charge of this project. I will continue to seek your advice about possible ways to make things better. Should things not work out I'll not hang up and kill myself. I will (as best I can) graciously accept defeat. But until such comes about I'm going to keep on chippin' away in order to reach my goal.

One more thing. I received a notice that you sent me a "doll". I hope it is one of those blow-up dolls. EEEEEEEEEEEEEEEK!!! In your letter you wrote that you "didn't want to spook me". But you did scare the shit out of me.

About writing to me. There is no need for you to use a lot of your time and energy writing lots of letters to me. You have a zillion things to do for your clients, your boss and yourself. Take it easy. Write me once a month. That will be okay with me. I'm okay and will continue to be okay. Don't worry about me. Gotta go!

Your lifelong light-skinned colored guy!
TEEEEEEEEEEEEEEEEEEEEEEEEEEEEEEEEOOOOOOOOOOOOOOOOOOOOOOH!

April 28, 2005

Pablo!

As of April 27th, there is $16.25 in my account. Not enough to keep our program moving forward.

Strange you mentioned Ben Affleck in your letter. Eek! Also strange is the fact that I saw the film <u>My Friend Flicka</u> when I was young!! No shit! Man, what is going on with our crazy-ass friendship? Many times, you'll write something that I've experienced, e.g. old black-and-white comedy on TV, my interest in art, travel, music, knowing Howard & Roz, ACLU, helping people, etc. You sure keep me on my toes. It helps me to survive in this hell-hole.

The weather has been very cold around here. Three weeks ago the heat was turned OFF. Everyone, prisoners, guards, (male & female) hospital staff, and all "de" folks (male and female) who work here complained to the new black warden. After the lockdown he ordered that the heat be turned on. Living with 2,000 prisoners and app. 700–800 employees when cold increased the tension and stress levels tenfold. I cannot adjust to cold weather. I almost froze to death in Korea. I hope the heat will stay on for many more weeks, at least until the weather becomes warmer.

Man, I'm worn out reorganizing things in this cage, plus trying to help keep the peace. I hear so many complaints about all kinds of issues. I cannot solve all the fucking problems prisoners have. Many men wrongly assume I do not have any problems. I'm writing this via pen in hand because I'm too worn out to type any more today. I'm going to lay down and sleep for 4 days. Well maybe not that long, but it will be at least 8–9 hours.

Behave yourself. Good luck reading that 900-page book Dougie sent you.

Better you than me. I'm outta here!
Tiyo

May 5, 2005

Yo Pablo!

Thank you a big loving bunch for the money! You have saved our program. All the guys, my crew and students send their strong words of appreciation to you. I shared your pictures and spoke about who you are and our friendship. The one gay student asked, "If Pablo isn't married tell him I'm available!" We all cracked up laughing!

I'll have things up and running in a few days. Check the enclosed. The word is out that I'm helping prisoners to read and write, seek GEDs and college courses. The prison "search team" (two very dumb rednecks) searched this cage and did not find anything illegal. So they said, "You're the guy teaching, eh?" They picked up Howard's letter and said, "You do too much reading and writing. We're going to put a halt to that shit!" I did not say anything. Next day I talked with the security captain. He told me not to worry, that the letter would be returned and for me to continue helping the men because it makes his job a lot easier! I think he chewed out the stupid-ass rednecks. I have to be careful because not all the guards and staff are pro-education supporters for prisoners. However, the majority of guards are in favor of our program. We lead by our deeds and actions. All the students are well-behaved. We are making positive progress and history at this prison. The students trust me and I trust and respect them. I enjoy working with and watching them grow in becoming better human beings. I'm trying to develop strong future leaders who will return to their

communities and put into practice their newly found skills, talents and education. Okay----gotta go! Don't worry about me. I plan to live to be 100. I'll be with you in spirit during the May 14, 2005, affair honoring Congresswoman Barbara Lee. You are indeed an amazing and loving guy. Hang in there!

Best wishes,
Tiyo

May 12, 2005

Hola Pablo,

It's back to my old trusty typewriter. I can hear your sigh of relief emanating from deep within your lungs. I should continue to punish you with my printing. But alas my mind instructs me to be just a bit more civil with you. Now to the business at hand. I want to cover some strange and not so strange things, e.g. being asked to sit at the bedside of a dying prisoner and the dream I had about my sister. So brace yourself.

I have regrouped our education program and we are up and running. Now that the weather is slowly warming up, we will move some parts of our program outside in the main yard. Such will allow the men who are not working in the sweatshops to attend during the mornings. The evening classes are for men who work during the day. This will also allow some men who reside on the other side of the prison to become involved in our program.

We will organize in 4–5 groups of 20–25 men in each group. Two of my crew will share instruction of each group. I will float around to each group listening, learning, and helping to answer a few questions. We have no problem attracting students. In prison news travels with the speed of light. We accept all who ask. Entrance exams not required! Free tuition! I'm hoping more gay guys will become involved. I'll explain my reason for wanting that to happen. We shall see what we shall see. By the way, hell no, I'm not entertaining any thoughts of becoming gay!

Next, the deathbed watch. Upon his arrival here a young white guy was placed in the hospital. He was infected with AIDS. Last year his condition became worse. About 2–3 months ago one of the male nurses sent word to me that the guy wanted to talk to me. Old dumbass me said "okay". The following week I went to the hospital and met him. He said he had heard about me from the prisoners who work in the hospital cleaning the floors and carrying out the trash and helping to bathe the patients, etc.

He begins telling me his life story, e.g. where he was born, dropped out of school during 7th grade, father physically and mentally abused him and his mother left home and started hanging with older guys, started drinking and using drugs, living in the streets, began stealing and burglarizing homes, and became a male prostitute, got beat up a lot. He has lost contact with his mother and two sisters and does not receive visits, nor mail. He has no friends on the outside nor at this prison. He did not tell me all this in one setting. It took weeks of me listening to him. I've become a good listener.

Each time I would visit him I would bring extra fruit, juices, milk, veggies, books and magazines, and the NY Times, and the pictures you sent me. I gave him my old radio. He enjoyed talking about music and how he wanted to become a guitar player. He would sometimes start to cry when accepting such items. Things were going along well and he seemed to become a bit better. Then lo and behold the fucking "lockdown" happened. Days later I was told he died. I was called to the hospital to pick up my radio and books. The nurse told me he asked her to thank me for the gifts and for bringing peace and friendship into his life.

Man, I've been a bit fucked up ever since. Hell of a sad and tragic way to die. To die in prison without family or friends is beyond my sense of reality. Prison and poverty take a heavy toll on prisoners and their families. I hope you don't mind me dumping all this crazy shit on you.

I think I mentioned that most prisoners, guards and staff wrongly assume that I do not have any problems. They think I'm able to resolve all sorts of conflicts. There are times when I feel as if my mind is about to explode. I need to unload just like most other folks. I guess writing to you is sort of like time for my personal catharsis. Guess what? I miss talking and listening to the guy.

I think it best if I postpone relaying the story about the dream I had about my sister. It was both beautiful and sad. My mood has changed since beginning this letter. I'm going to take a walk outside. I need to take in some outside air and mother nature. I'll be in touch soon again. Hang in there my lifelong friend. Thank you for allowing me to talk to you today.

Sincerely,
Tiyo

May 18, 2005

Yo Pablo, my lifelong soulful paleface brother!!

I've been incarcerated for 30 years. No one, not even my sister whom I love very much, has ever offered to write a letter to the warden expressing concern for my welfare and my work with prisoners. You fuckin' floored me! You continue to overpower me with your incessant kindness and rock-solid support. I first read and then pressed your letter to my chest and repeated the words. "Oh, thank you, Pablo---thank you---I will never forget your kindness and support---I'm forever beholden to you---I love you my friend. I love you!" I am deeply moved. Man, you are truly something else!!

Now listen up! I devised a surreptitious counter strategy that will protect our educational supplies and my own stuff. Two of my crew members (both are in the new college program and doing well) are assigned as janitors and runners in the staff building. They carry and deliver mail and memos to staff members everywhere in the prison. The staff building is one of the very few places not to be searched. The guard in charge of the building is one of the few guards who supports our program. He gave us the old "wink and nod" to allow storage and access to our supplies whenever needed. In short, all is taken care of and we are up and running. My personal and important things are in a safe place. The name of the game in prison is often called the cat-and-mouse game. Oftentimes we have to outsmart the guards and staff. Some prisoners engage in negative games. We stay on the road to positive goals.

I also want to explain when something happens here, e.g. escapes, killings, major fights between guards and prisoners, the warden contacts the commissioner who is in Harrisburg, PA, which is the state capital, and requests more guards to bring control to the prison. The commissioner relays word to other prisons to send their Corrections Emergency Response Teams (CERT) to SCI-Dallas. The regular guards who work here are not permitted to join the CERT during the search because they could be tempted to protect certain prisoners from being searched by telling the CERT squad, "This prisoner is okay, leave him and his stuff alone." The CERT guys look at all of us as the same. Their orders are trash and bash and get out. Searches come with the territory. There is nothing can be done about it. Prisoners will be involved with dope, weapons, sex, stealing, etc. as long as prisons exist.

I truly appreciate your willingness to write to the warden (no need to do so) on my behalf. What happened to me also happened to 2,000 other prisoners. They didn't single me out. Some prisoners got beat up and placed in "the Hole". We all caught hell. You asked why I don't get sucked into such negative shit. Well, it's because of what I've learned from people like you, Howard, my sister and my determination to turn my life round and try to become a positive and productive person. I refuse to go negative. I will only fight in self-defense. Nor will I ever give up on myself. I want to change my life and also help change the corrupt criminal justice system and save a few lives before I die. I don't want to be thought of as a saint or hero. Fuck that shit. I'm just me. Take it or leave it. I like me much better than I did years ago. I've not reached my goal on self-improvement. I still have a temper and dislike evil people, racism, sexism, wars, fuckin' prisons, the list goes on and on. I don't want to be perfect. I just want to be at peace with myself.

Soooooooooooooo don't worry about me. I plan to live to be 100! Yip—peeeeeeeeeeeeeeee! You'd be surprised to learn that I am one strong mentally and physically smartass light-skin motherfucker!

Love you madly,
TEEEEEEEEEEEEEEEEEEEEEEEEEOOOOOOOOOOOOOOOH!

July 7, 2005 [First letter of the day]

Yo big **"P"**,

Received and read yet another of your fucked-up letters informing me that you were waiting at Starbucks to talk with Gore Vidal. Little wonder you're never home when I call! Now you're off to Paris to get laid. You made clear your lust for Diane Lane to have a divorce. I too want her to have a divorce so that she and I can get married. (Hallelujah!)

I was and still am surprised to learn about the pending operations on your hip, knee and later your shoulder. That's some heavy shit! (Whew!) Don't you dare tell me not to worry about your sorry white ass. I already started! You sure know how to fuck up my day. I've not had any major operations on my high yellow narrow ass. However, rheumatoid arthritis in my lower back and hips, along with incessant and increasing hypertension and age, has made my pain have pain. So what? Fuck it!! We march onward and upward. Two slightly wounded intellectual kooks trying to help save some lives and bring about positive change. Only insane people chart such a crazy course. Keep me posted regarding your situation. I'll send two black hookers each week to saturate you with pussy and help you recuperate. Believe me black pussy is smokin'!! Remember what it did to Jesse Jackson and Bill Cosby. (Ha Ha Ha!)

Hey, Hey, Hey, Hey! Thanks a big lovin' bunch for ordering Jazz Times and Downbeat magazines. Such will help me to learn what's what and who's who in the jazz world. By the way, did I inform you that app. 2–3 years ago someone, I never found out who, sent my name to the folks at "Who's Who"? I received the forms etc. and a notice that I would be accepted. I thought to myself, why would they consider having an old black prisoner in Who's Who? It did not make sense to me. I wrote a "thank you no thanks" letter to them. Yet they continued sending letters requesting I reconsider. I stopped responding to their letters. The only person I think would submit my name is of course Howard Zinn. I did not think it appropriate to ask him. I forgot about it until today.

I completed reading the book <u>Progressive Hollywood</u>. The book has had a profound eye-opening and thought-provoking effect on my overall thinking and plans for the future. Later on I will write you a blow-by-blow review of the book. For now let me just say (write) that I'm going to try harder to fight the powers that be! My mind is spinning with ideas, so much so that I <u>must</u> ask for your advice. I want to write a book about the development of the underdevelopment of incarcerated women and men. I want to put the prison system in the U.S. on trial in a manner that prisoners, their friends/families/supporters and most importantly everyday folks in America will understand and maybe become involved in the struggle against building more prisons. I want to explain some of the ways war, poverty and crime are used by the powers that be to eat poor people of color as daily food. In my view, most people do not fully understand that once inside these hell-holes, the system is geared to program/develop prisoners to reoffend again and again. My questions to you are am I being too emotional about this due to reading the book? Am I over my head regarding even thinking about writing a book? I want to try to do something good in my life before leaving this world. I want to do something that others can maybe use to fight the system and hopefully win.

Reading and learning about snitching Kazan touched a tender nerve because of what my nephew did to me. I still cannot understand how a person becomes a snitch. If I have a serious argument with a guy, I'd rather first try to resolved the matter peacefully. If that does not work, then let's settle it the old-fashion way, e.g. one on one physically. Fuck turning the guy or the matter over to the powers that be. I still cannot understand how and why a person becomes a snitch. I don't have it in me to become such an asshole. Enough of this dumb shit.

I gotta relay the story of the 4th of July watermelon caper that happened here at SCI-Dallas. At app. 6:45 a.m. on the 4th of July the announcement was made over the PA system that "during the noon meal a special meal of hamburger, hot dogs, mashed potatoes, baked beans, store-bought rolls, butter, salad, tomatoes and onions, cookies, soda and a special treat, **watermelon**, will be served." The guys on the cellblocks gave a loud and long cheer. During the breakfast meal most of the guys are smiling and talking shit about how glad they were about getting some watermelon. Everything moves along well and it's a warm day and most of the guys go out to the yard. Others stay in the cells looking at TV, or listening to radios, or just sleeping. Not many guys spend much time reading or writing. At 10:30 a.m. a call is made over the PA system for all kitchen workers to report to work. This is the regular work schedule and routine. They are required to wear white shirts and pants and white paper hats. When they arrived at the chow hall they eat first and later help feed the main lines. Everything is going along okay then one of the most crazy events happens. A Hispanic guy who does not work in the kitchen puts on white pants and shirt and joins the kitchen workers as they walk into the chow hall. The kitchen staff of 4–5 men and one woman are busy checking other things, e.g. trays, spoons, etc., and do not look at all the workers coming into the kitchen. The guy sneaks into the back of the kitchen, goes in the freezer and steals a very large watermelon, puts it in a large mop bucket along with two mops and wheels it out of the mess hall, past the Control Area, past the guards who wrongly assume he is a kitchen worker. He heads towards the cellblock that he is assigned to. As he pushes the mop bucket he looks back, to see if any guards are following him. Guess what? He trips. The mop bucket tips over and out rolls the watermelon. The guards in the towers zero in on him with the high-powered cameras and call Control. Guards come running and surround the guy and asked the man where did he get the watermelon? He says, "No speak de English!" He refused to tell, so they put cuffs on him and take him to the "Hole". They charge him with stealing state property and give him 15 days in the "Hole" plus charge him $25.95 for the watermelon. The guards then put the watermelon in the center of the yard and place a sign in the watermelon, "Watermelon Not for Sale or to Eat!" Everyone was laughing, even the guards that caught the guy were laughing. Truly amazing!

Let me end on a positive note. I truly enjoy meeting and growing to know you and striving hard to earn your trust, respect and lifelong friendship. I've learned many positive and happy things from you. You have helped me become a better person and never to give up regardless of the odds against me. I am proud to know you and to be one of your many friends. I wish you tons of positive blessings and many bright moments.

Your one and only high yellow handsome colored guy who can out type your sorry ass,
TEEEEEEEEEEEEEEEEEEEEEEEOH!

July 7, 2005 [Second letter of the day]

Pablo,

120 of us were moved to "F" block which is located <u>outside</u> the main building. We must walk a long way before reaching the hospital, chow hall, gym, etc. Seven guys helped carry my things. That's the reason I need a trunk because within 3–4 months we have to move back to slow death row. This has been a truly fucked-up 10–12 days for me. I'm now in a <u>smaller</u> cage that has 2 bunks. It's hard to turn around, plus the smell & dirt are outrageous! And it's fucking hot! Plus, the hot water was turned off for 4 days. We are all catching hell.

Tiyo

COMMONWEALTH OF PENNSYLVANIA
Department of Corrections
SCI-Dallas

July 07, 2005

SUBJECT: MOVEMENT TO F BLOCK

TO: TO ALL I BLOCK INMATES

FROM: Joseph Semon
Unit Manager, Unit V

All inmates on I block will be temporarily moving to F block this weekend to facilitate maintenance on I Block.

All cell property (cell curtains, mattresses etc.) must be taken.

I do not have an expected date of return at this time.

JS/smb

Pablo,

→ DO NOT Return This To me!

120 of us were moved To "F" block which is located outside The main building. We must walk a long way before reaching The hospital, Chow hall, gym, etc. Seven guys helped carry my Things. That's the reason I need A Trunk because within 3-4 months we have To move back To slow death row, This has been A Truly Fucked up 10-12 days for me. I'm now in A smaller cage That has 2 bunks. It's hard To Turn Around! Plus The smell + dirt Are outrageous! And its Fucking hot! Plus The hot water was Turned off for 4 days! We Are All catching hell, Tuyo

July 18, 2005

Soulful greetings my friend,

I just received and read your July 14th letter. I want you to know that I think about you every day! I even talk to the two pictures I have of you. Yes, I admit to saying your name each time I pray. I'm a bit off balance emotionally because I know you are physically hurting from the operations on your knee and hip. It's hard for me to tease and act silly when my close friend is hurting. Sorry I dumped all the negative news about my problems on you when you are hurting. It's been only four days ago that the surgery took place. Yes, yes, yes, I worry about you and the cats. Okay, okay, okay I'm a pussy!! So what? I can't help it! Hell of a thing to say (write) from a prisoner who is sentenced to "life". Many people wrongly assume that all prisoners are scum and hardcore killers. Phil and Del Africa and even old-ass me are not that at all. There is a lot of good inside us. That our friendship is built on a solid foundation of mutual trust, respect, openness, positive craziness, concern, compassion and love. That's why if you stump your toe it affects me too. I feel this way about our friend Howard Zinn. You guys have made and continue to make a profound positive influence on me and my outlook on life and people. You will never know how much I truly wish I could be there to help with the chores, open doors, escort you from place to place, make you laugh and read scripts. And most importantly, load up the hooker!! ☺ Yes, I would become your one and only colored personal trainer. (See how easy teasing you is for me?) I tried to stay super serious and boom, all of a sudden something crazy pops into my mind to say (write) to you. Hey, I just noticed there are no paragraphs in this letter (eek!!) I just started writing from my heart. The east coast heat wave is alive and well here at SCI-Dallas. Temps for the past two weeks have been in the high 90s. Heat advisories given every day. The humidity is humming, and kickin' butt! Living in these small cages and dealing with the heat is pure hell. All the guys are wearing just boxer shorts, draping ourselves with cold wet towels. Add in the stench and dirt and you'll have a good idea of our living conditions. But check this out. All the offices of the staff members are air-conditioned. Even the guard towers are air-conditioned. The hospital is not!! Amazing, eh?

I'm eating a lot of oranges, drinking lots of water, milk, Tang, and tea. I don't eat too much food. Guess that's why I'm on the thin side. I'm not into eating junk foods or pork products. No, I'm not Jewish!! Hey, I made a paragraph!

Before closing this missive, I want to make clear that I now realize that I made a mistake sending you all that bad news during the time of your surgery. Please take it easy. Get lots of rest and good foods. No need for you to write me until you are fully recovered. Save your strength. Focus on healing! I'll do the writing! So be cool!! No more sending bad news to you.

The guys and I are happy to learn you are pleased with our "homemade" card. They tease me by saying you are the only

Hollywood agent who has an agent (me)! We had fun putting it together for you. You help create many bright moments for us. And as you well know I love messing with your mind.

I confident with all the strong loving support you are receiving from family friends, fellow workers and prisoners, you'll recover well and be up and running about more than ever before. I'll always stay in touch.

Warm hugs and much love,
The Grasshopper!

July 29, 2005

Dear Tiyo:

I'm truly sorry to hear what you and your fellow prisoners are going through right now. Someone of lesser spirit and strength would not be able to take it, and I'm sure there are guys who break under that kind of stress.

I received Monty Neill's "Preface" and I think it's excellent. I have sent that and the whole manuscript to my brother, who is going to get it put on a disk, and then make sure it is formatted in the right way to send to iUniverse to get it published. It will be an exciting moment when it comes off the press, bound, and ready to distribute!

Do take care of yourself. Roslyn and I send love,

Howard

September 7, 2005

Dear Pablo,

Stayed up damn near all last night until I regained better control of myself. Yesterday while talking to you via the phone I broke down. It was the first time during the 30 years of being incarcerated that my emotions got the best of me. It was the first time for Joe Semon to witness my weakness. This morning he came by this cage to check on me. I thanked him, told him "I'm okay!" We shook hands, smiled at each other and wished each other well. It just so happens that this cage is located near his office. He has a lot of power at this prison. He is the "unit manager" in charge of approximately 400 prisoners, 4 counselors, 20 guards, and 2 female secys. He has the power to move, transfer, and place prisoners in "the Hole". When he became aware that a staff member called me a "nigger convict" he called me to his office to discuss the matter because he assumed I would attack the staff person. Word had reached him that the staff person was informed that I was preparing to confront and become physically involved with the staff member. Joe told me to "hold on" and not say or do anything until he investigated the situation and got back with me. He suggested I stay in this cage until he checked things out. In sum, I took his advice, plus did a lot of personal soul-searching. My main "crew members" and all our students were going to get involved physically if the guards came after me. As time and days passed, I cooled down. I realized it would have been impossible to win fighting the guards. Nor did I want my crew or our students to risk their lives, and lose the chance to make parole and be released from this hell-hole. I bit the bullet and we are better off, reorganizing in a positive way. They are unaware that yesterday I broke down.

Long ago I had hopes of talking with you, teasing the hell out of you, giving you a hard time, and making you laugh and happy. The voice you listened to was not the normal sound of my voice. With tears running down my face, nose running and unable to speak clearly my introduction to you was a disaster. I implore your understanding. In the future you will hear my voice at its very best. You heard me when I was weak. I want you to hear me when I'm strong, in control of myself. I have the courage and confidence in myself to admit to my mistakes and when I mess up and admit to you that I'm not the assumed strong person people think I am. However, I always try hard to recover and rebuild what I may have lost. I have opened up to you, stripped myself bare to my bones and allowed you see and learn about the inner me, my emotions, pain and hurt. No holding back. I've not been this upfront with Howard, whom you know I truly love and respect. You have become my sole outlet for my true emotions. Living in this prison for 30 years has taken a toll on my mind, body, and soul. Yet my spirit grows ever stronger. It's a strange inner feeling that drives me not to give up without trying to make a strong comeback. During past years I've witnessed men self-destruct, hang up, jump off the top range to their death. Others have died in their sleep, others waiting and wanting to die walking around in a daze. It's sad and tragic. I refuse to stop trying to become a better person.

Thank you very much for everything!
Tiyo

Hope your hip and knee are healing well. Let me know when you're fully recovered because I'll race you to the length of the pool!

Next time I'll write re: my thoughts about Bush and the slow-ass response to the hurricane that hit the Gulf Coast. Stay tuned!!

September 27, 2005

Some good news!!

Joe Semon called me to his office, shook my hand and expressed his appreciation of the card you sent him. It was the first time for him to receive a thank you card from a prisoner's family or friend. Also, it was the first time a call came to this prison from someone in California seeking information about the general welfare of a prisoner. He asked me to be the facilitator for the character development classes (see enclosed). I've been asked to draw up some plans regarding expanding the activities for men over 50 years of age. At the present time, weightlifting is being offered. I think board games such as chess, dominos, checkers, Scrabble, cards, ping-pong, volleyball, half-court basketball, Monopoly, etc. would in my view give the men more to choose from. Soon, I won't be able to do much of anything, much less lift weights.

Some really good news! The cellblock guard just handed me your recent (and I might add long-awaited) letter. Holy Shit!! I'm sitting on the bunk with a big shit-eating grin on my face. Talk about great timing! Wow! Some strange powerful force must be at work regarding our relationship and lifelong friendship. I just wrote two songs, "Boot in the Butt" and "Living a Life of Love" (I'm mailing them to you and dedicating them to you). The tune "Boot in the Butt" is about the hell I had to deal with regarding the racist remark that was directed at me by a redneck SCI-Dallas Klan staff member. I felt like someone had kicked me in my ass. More later about this situation. The tune "Living a Life of Love" is especially about people like you and Howard and all the progressive Hollywood folks. I am against wars, racism, prisons, sexism, abuse of children, rape, all forms of violence, yes, even murder. I'm all for peace, love, earthy sex, humor, great music, great foods, kindness, mutual trust and respect. I want you to know that although there are some guards and staff members here who hate my guts, the majority of staff members like and respect me. I help a lot of people, guards and prisoners, and I feel good doing it. **I happen to like me very much**!

Back to your fucked-up letter. Yes, I too was very very happy to hear your voice. I would totally be at ease being around you, teasing and giving you a hard time. You would also witness how I go about getting things done. I work hard for long hours in an organized and efficient manner. I used to fuck women the same way!

Glad "de" cats are fine. I'm sure they are not looking down the nine-year road re: "cat mitzvahs". Don't you dare start writing to me in Hebrew! (Fucking showoff!) I speak nothing but world-class hi-falutin' light-skinned coloredism!

Hey! I'm happy to learn your dad is doing okay. I am also pleased to know that you are once again donating platelets, especially as it appears you have an extra-large number in your blood. I always knew you were full of shit. I was surprised you were also full of something good. Knowing what you're doing I just may remove "the spell" I put on your sorry ass and allow you to gain a ho! ☺

What's with the "maybe" will buy a motorcycle? Please be careful.

Please, please, give my greetings and a hug to Howard Zinn before or after the soiree. I'll be with y'all (via the airwaves) during the entire evening. If you feel someone push you it'll be me.

Great time to let you know that I'm not only broke but I asked all the guys to loan me their monthly pay for our two programs. I would like to soon repay them. These mofos will kill a rock. You wouldn't want me to get beat up would you? Eek! The men trust me and they know if I give my word all will be okay. You will have to get up off your lazy ass, drive to the bank in order to save my old ass.

You'll soon receive a package of materials and another letter from me in a day or two. Thanks for the article re: cost of phone calls from prisoners. It's the main reason I do not make many phone calls. I've called Howard Zinn just one time in 22 years. Oh, by the way, make sure the publisher does not send my book here. Such would cause big big problems for me. I'll explain in my next letter. Want you to know I'm feeling much much better and ready and able to fuck with you for at least another 20–40 years! Take a long hit on the hookah and dedicate it to me!! Ahhhh, yes! Thanks muchly!

Tiyo

"A boot in The butt"

(Solo on Rhythm changes)

October 24, 2005

Hi Pablo,

Okay, okay, okay, O-fucking-K! I've been as big of a dickhead as you regarding our normal (nothing is normal about us or our situations) exchange of fucked-up letters. I will use the same lame-ass "no excuse" you laid on me. Don't get me wrong. I'm not at all complaining. I have been blessed to have a keen/acute sense of understanding of the flow of emotions, interests, work ethics, activities, health, etc. of people close to me and whom I love and respect. Sounds crazy, eh? Well check this out. I can sense when things are going good and not so good for you, e.g. with certain people you deal with, organizing events and trying to make sure everything is okay, checking with your mom and dad, arranging and rearranging your crazy schedule, waiting in line at airports to be searched/scanned, spending time with Prima and Hep Cat, visiting sets, yoga, and dealing with my sorry light-skin ass. You know lots of people, right? Lots of people think they know you but do not take time to know who you really are and what makes you tick, e.g. things that inspire you, interest you, things that piss you off, things you love and appreciate. Many folks don't know much about your history growing up, travel and the good and rough experiences during your life. I mention this now because if it is to be that we never meet face to face or again talk via the phone all will be okay with me. There will be peace between us come what may. Things are cool between us so be cool regarding writing to me. Since I have more time on my hands than you'll ever have, allow me to do the bulk of the writing.

Now to "de" K-razy good and bad news. During the past 3 1/2 weeks the weather has been rainy and extremely cold which in turn made this hell-hole really cold. The "no heat until November 1st" policy was in effect. Prisoners and guards were wearing long johns, coats, wool hats, etc. The only places that had heat were the hospital, kitchen, Control Area, the offices of the warden and the two deputies, the sweatshops and shower rooms. Well, things became so cold that the women who work mostly on the night shift began to raise hell. Then the 6 a.m. to 2 a.m. joined the call for the heat to be turned on. Lo and behold on October 20th the heat was turned on. Credit the "hos!" who had the gonads to get the "balls" rolling in the "hot" direction. Also, news is out that the black warden will retire in 1–2 years. Most wardens stay on the job for 10–25 years. Not this homeboy. He is preparing to flee de scene!

The article in the NY Times re: lifers in PA had a negative impact on most of the 430 "lifers" at this prison. Some have given up and lost the desire to push on and create/reorganize their lives, learn new things, e.g. computers, Spanish, art, music and so on. They need to keep their minds active and challenge themselves. Thank goodness there are strong men who have said "fuck 'em, we're moving on to the courts and the study of law." These men will never give up. They are still able to work, play, laugh, exercise and greet each other with a smile. Each new day is a special day in their lives. They face their death with profound courage.

The issue of dying brings to mind the not knowing if my sister Bette is still alive or not. The guy who moved in with Bette's daughter Odetta at Bette's house has in the past physically abused Odetta, e.g. tied her with duct tape and sexually abused her. She has been an alcoholic for many years and now may be addicted to drugs. The last time I heard from her was approximately a year ago when she called here drunk and angry and left a message for me not to write or call her or Bette. It's one hell of a sad and tragic mess. The not knowing if Bette is alive or dead is at times difficult for me to deal with.

The classes are going very well. The guys who signed your birthday card are in the program. I've asked each student to lead the discussions for one week. That helps the men in public speaking, teaching, etc. I strive to help the men to take charge of their learning and thinking and put it into practice and discover self-empowerment. At first some were a bit shy standing and speaking to the group. Once they adjust to the situation they become better at the task. For most of the guys it was the first time they became both student and teacher.

Hey, don't forget to remind Howard to relay word to the publisher not to send a copy of the book to me. As long as you, Howard and others receive a copy all will be okay. Regarding calling you......if a crisis pops up, I'll try to call you. If not, don't sweat it. I'll always stay in touch via the written word and "airwaves"! Both your phone numbers are on my approved phone list. I'll factor in the difference in time and your crazy wake-up and work schedules. Stay alert!

My health is hanging tough for a 74-year-old dude. I can still get around very well. My blood pressure is difficult to control and the arthritis in my back and hips slows me down a bit. No big deal! I plan to be around many more years so that I can help you pull yourself up by the bootstraps and into a decent well-paying job.

Gotta tell you about my first-ever experience of listening to and enjoying Yiddish music. Last weekend the Philly Temple University jazz/classical station, which is on 24/7, featured a group named "Counterpoint", led by Robert De Corya (I'm not at all sure of the correct spelling of his name). They sing a cappella. The music was a mix of Jewish songs sung/created in the camps during the Holocaust. Many of the songs were in a minor key and sung at various tempos, e.g. very slow, and up-tempo happy dancing music. I did not understand a word being sung but enjoyed the flow, colors, mood, harmony, texture and feelings expressed by the singers. I strongly recommend you check them out and let me know what you think of the music.

Enough rap for now. Get back to your work. I'll catch you soon again. Hang in there! Continue to be kind and loving to the cats.

TEEEEEEEEEEE-TOE

Oh, by the way. I expect a formal invitation to the next seder!

*Pablo,

The prison will not allow me to receive the book The New Abolitionists. The book contains one of my essays re: abolishing prison. I'd like you to order the book, read it, take pictures of the front and back covers and send photos to me. It's a way for me to see the book and also learn (from your review) what the other writers think about abolishing prisons.

Tiyo

2006
"AT LEAST WE'RE NOT IN DARFUR"

January 25, 2006

Dear Pablo,

I need to "talk" to you regarding two very emotional events that took place yesterday. I implore your understanding. I need to vent and let my true feelings/emotions flow freely.

I received the enclosed letter that created joy and sadness. Briefly—George is the father of one of our students, and I say <u>our</u> students because I always explain to the men that you are the one who started our education program. I share your pictures and some, but not all, of your crazy/happy sayings. His son, Cookie was one of if not the best of the best students. Easy to teach, and quick to learn. He became my main back up. I placed him in my jazz group playing keyboard. He had "it" to play music and sports. Guys nicknamed him "Tiyo the 2nd"! He <u>changed</u> and <u>turned</u> his life around from drugs and other nefarious activities, into a positive take charge sort of life.

I helped him make parole and get a gig with a construction company, plus a spot in a jazz group. He had saved enough money to visit his dad in Cal. They had a fine time together. It was the last time for them to be together. Cookie returned to Pittsburgh and within 6–7 months died. He had Lou Gehrig's disease. He never told me. Nor did he ever complain. Cookie was his dad's favorite son. I've been trying to cheer up George but in fact I'm more fucked up than he is. I hide my pain and emotions from everyone but you. What happened next really fucked me up.

Do you remember the story about the young white kid who was being pressured by a sick-ass Negro, whom my crew had to talk to before he <u>accidentally fell down the steps</u>? Well, the young kid is doing great and has gained praise and respect from his peers and staff. He comes to my cage and tells me his life story, viz. hard time growing up, no father, trouble in school, got into drugs, stealing, etc. Then he says he would like me to be his dad! And that because I'm sentenced to life and will die here he would give anything in order to take my place and allow me to go home! Man, that really got to me. Still does. I retreat to this cage and write to you. I don't want the men to see me during times of weakness. Please believe me I'm not the strong person people assume I am. I hurt deep inside. I now have to walk out of this hell-hole cage and talk to guys who want to get involved with our program. Hell of a way for me to live.

Tiyo

February 23, 2006

Yo Pablo!

The guys informed me re: NY Times. I forgot to relay word to you. I have a good crew of guys who look after me and help keep things moving in a positive direction.

Yesterday, I received word that I am scheduled for an interview with the "inmate program manager" re: becoming involved with organizing and teaching a new program called "ethics". I also learned that word concerning my conduct and the work that I do to help prisoners has reached the warden and his staff. The suggestion that I would be a good candidate to teach came from Joe Semon, the unit manager, who allowed me to talk with you on the phone. He and I get along very well. If the "ethics" class takes too much of my time away from teaching civil and criminal law, I'll stick with teaching law classes. Whatever happens, I'll keep you posted. Stay tuned!

In my view, what is really needed, not just here but in all prisons, are prisoners of all races to become positive role models/leaders. Prisoners are more relaxed and willing to listen to and learn from another prisoner whom they eat & sleep with every day. It works positive & negative. But the strong ones make history and earn self-empowerment & self-determination. Each time I help a guy excel it fills my heart with joy. Teasing your sorry ass also brings joy into my heart.

Teeeeee-O

3/7/06

Yo Pablo! :)

Brief update.

Received NY Times;

① How did you do RE: "OSCARS"?

② I've selected 15 of our Top students For our CRIMINAL and civil law classes. You. They are REALLY excited About learning about the law, courts, etc.

④ Don't let anything but or ANYONE EVER hold you back From happen... Carrying For others And helping bring some PEACE And justice in The world!

I'll Always stay in Touch.

Hugs + much love,

Tiyo

March 3, '06

Dear Tiyo—

Good to hear from you. My brother is working on the publication of yours memoir. It's a slow process, but I assure you, it will

Pablo, like you, is grateful that you two have become friends. You're both exceptional human beings.

Love,

Howard

:)

April 4, 2006

Dear Tiyo

Great news that you have an essay in the new book on prisons!

I hope to give you news soon on the publication of your book.

Love from me & Ros ———

Howard

Also, the new court decision on lifers is encouraging! How I wish you can benefit from that, along with others. Keep me informed.

April 6, 2006

Dear Tiyo:

We are about to send your memoir to the publisher, and have a last chance to make any changes you want to make.

So here's a question. I've noticed that you slide very quickly in your memoir over your state trial and sentence to life imprisonment. The reader is bound to want to know more. What exactly were you charged with? Whose murder? What was the evidence against you? What kind of defense did your lawyer put up? What happened at the trial?

Maybe you'd rather not go into this. But if you do, let me know, and we'll add whatever you want to the story.

In any case, it won't be long before your memoir will be in print!

Love,
Howard

April 13, 2006

Hola Amigo!

Como esta usted?

You have influenced my life in numerous ways. So much so that in my weak moments, I have picked up some of your fucked-up habits, e.g. (a) not making excuses for not writing to family and friends, (b) taking on seemingly impossible tasks, e.g. teaching and helping people to better understand and challenge the present political and legal systems, (c) teasing Howard and Roz.

Now to the bizarre happenings here at the SCI-Dallas Palace. Due to two unrelated incidents, this hell-hole was locked down this past Sunday, April 9th. It appears that four or five prisoners on "C" block tested positive for, of all things, chicken pox. They were placed in the isolated ward of the hospital. C block was then locked down. When the rest of the prisoners returned from the noon meal, which by the way featured of all things CHICKEN, all cellblocks were locked down. News arrived that a prisoner who was in the "Hole" set fire to his cell. As the fire and smoke filled the cellblock the guards pulled the switches and opened the cell doors. Out came the prisoners running towards the exit doors. The guards at first attempted to stop the prisoners. Fights began between the guards and prisoners. Due to the heavy smoke some guards began running towards the exit doors. Two or three guards passed out from smoke inhalation. Waiting outside the exit doors were squads of state police with guns and vans, a local fire company, and ambulances from the local hospital. Within an hour or so things were cleaned up and the all clear given. The prison stayed locked down until after the evening meal. At 6 p.m. the call "Yard Out" came and the prisoners hauled ass to the yard. C block remains locked down until April 29th.

With all the negativity going on around here there is also small bits of positive news regarding some prisoners studying and staying out of trouble and remaining on a positive path. Such is our groovy group of guys. For us class time appears to zoom by. The discussions are lively, informative and interesting. The men enjoy reading, researching cases and critically analyzing various legal points of views. I enjoy being around them and cheering them on. They help me to learn new things. I've set things up in such a way that each man is both a teacher and a student. Of the 15 students, I think 10 will become strong jailhouse lawyers. They keep me on my toes. Come September I'll evaluate our overall progress and make necessary adjustments that will improve our program. The men know about you and our crazy sorry-ass relationship. They always asked about you and have nick-named you and me "the fucked-up good guys"! I think some of them may well be on their way to becoming as fucked up as we are. Poor souls.

Okay, enough news for now. I've got to get busy answering the questions from Howard. And one more thing. Wherever you are and whatever you are doing, please know that for some strange but happy reason and feeling I love and respect you. Now that should surely prove without a doubt that I'm truly fucked up in the head. Take care my friend. I'll always stay in touch.

Your only light-skin colored badass MOFO friend!!!!!!!!!!

TEEEEEEEEEEEEEEEEEEEEEOOOOOOOOOOOOOOOOH!

May 16, 2006

Yo my homee PABLO! ☺

Received your beautiful card when you were roamin' around Roma. The flick of the Colosseo is impressively beautiful!! Thank you very much for thinking about me and taking time to send me truly wonderful cards as you travel to places in the world that I can only dream about. You bring tons of joy and inspiration into my life and my work.

Yesterday, I shared with the now 22 wide-eyed students your life's story along with photos of you, the cats ☺, your house, etc. It's the first time for the men to hear and learn who you are and your work and the amazing things you do to help bring about healing and positive change in the world. I've not told them that you are totally K-razy and in need of a class A blow job!

Now for a brief overview of "de" happenings here at the Dallas Palace.

(A) Our classes are going great. We started with 12 guys. We now have 22 dedicated students. I've expanded our program to include the reading of a book per month, plus the NY Times "Week in Review", front page stories, etc. We now have open, no-holds-barred discussions re: politics, the courts, prisons, the death penalty, wars, families & friends, dealing with anger/rage, seeking wise counsel, etc. I also have a half day of fun, e.g. music, jokes and relaxation. Each week I receive requests from guys wanting to join the class. We can only handle 22 at a time. The guys work together in teams of 4. By the way, the guards on this cellblock are aware of our classes. However they are pleased with the way the men conduct themselves. There is a lot more peace and understanding between prisoners and guards. I'm very proud of the men and their work. In the offing they will take my place. Yip-peeeee! ☺ I bought 20 small black law dictionaries, 50 legal pads, 15 reams of typing paper, 100 pens, 100 pencils, 50 typing ribbons, 10 small dictionaries, a typewriter for "Fingers" (the fast, fast, fast typing man). On the 4th of July, I would like to give a "surprise" sort of meeting for the guys, e.g. chips, sodas, candy bars, cheese & crackers, etc., plus give them a two-week break to relax. Such (hopefully) will help re-energize the men for the coming 4–5 months of study. Plus, I'd like to spend a bit of time writing and practicing music and of all things resting a bit. The men fail to realize that I'm no longer a "spring" chicken. Eek! ☺

(B) Received word from Howard re: publishing of my autobio. All should be completed soon. I explained the reasons why it would be best not to send a copy of the book to me. The new rules do not allow prisoners to write books. I would be placed in "the Hole" for a long period of time.

(C) I continue to be concerned about your father. I hope things are improving for him. Your mother, sister and, of course, your dad are in my daily thoughts and prayers. Yes, and you too!

Well, it's 2:30 a.m. and I'm a bit worn out. This is the first time I've not teased you re: your love life. I'll cut you a break this time. However, next time I contact you I'll put a hurtin' on your sorry ass. So stay alert!

Hope you're feeling good and hard at work making lots of bread because it's almost time to renew the NY Times.

Gotta go (to sleep!). Again---thanks for the many kind and powerful favors. I'm forever beholden to you. Long live love, good music & food, hip women and _____ (fill in "de" blank!). ☺

Tiyo

Seven of the dozens of incarcerated students Tiyo helped earn their GEDs at SC[...]

May 25, 2006

Pablo—

Today I received news that my sister Bette died. I've asked my Quaker friends Bev and Wally Williams to call you. Joe Semon will not be here until Tuesday May 30th. I hope he will allow me to call you. Sorry to send such news to you esp. when you are worried about your dad. I'm going to rest a bit. I'll be okay. I will continue teaching our students.

Tiyo

May 25, 2004

Pablo —

Today I received news that my sister Bette died. I've asked my Quaker friends, Bev and Wally Williams to call you. Joe Semons will not be here until Tuesday May 30th. I hope he will allow me to call you. Sorry to send such news to you esp. when you are worried about your dad. I'm going to rest ~~~~~~~ a bit.

I'll be okay. I will continue teaching our students.

June 1, 2006

Yo my lifelong lovable friend! ☺

It was <u>pure powerful positive timing</u> that placed me in Semon's office to receive your call. Man—something wonderful and beautiful is happening to us! Pure freakin' magic!! Whew! Thank you very much for being <u>with me</u> when I <u>truly need you.</u>

I accept your advice and have informed the men that I will shift and delegate more responsibility to the two men who have the needed drive, determination, & skills to become very good leaders both here and on the outside. I explained that although I'm 74 years old, I listen to and learn from people like you, Howard, et al. I took an in-depth inner evaluation of myself and asked why I tend to do so many things and take care of people and their problems. For the first time I "<u>opened up</u>" to the men, e.g. the times when I'm not strong; that I hurt more inside than most people; that I need more time to rest, read, write, listen to and play a bit of music, etc. I also told them about my sister Bette passing.

I'm confident that the men will become self-empowered and become positive role models here and outside in the streets. I enjoy helping the guys. Such helps me survive, thrive and stay alive!!

You asked me to send you the names of various staff members who have helped and continue to help me help many others. Brace yourself! ☺

Joe Ryan: He is the ex-superintendent/warden of this prison. He helped open doors that allowed me to complete my undergraduate and graduate programs, plus record an album of music (see enclosed) and kept the "redneck guards" off my back. He retired 4–5 years ago. However, his two sons work here, e.g. Lt. Ryan and Bobby Ryan. Plus, Joe comes to visit me once a year and we walk around the prison laughing & talking & teasing each other. When a crisis comes about I spend time with his sons, esp. Bobby. (He knows that I'm teaching 22 men.) He often tells me I've become not just a positive role model for prisoners to learn from but the father and teacher the men did not have when they were young and growing up. While talking with Bobby he mentioned that what I'm doing for the men should be replicated on a larger scale at most prisons. The major problem will be funding and finding/selecting prisoners to teach such subjects that the prison does not provide in the education department. Most wardens would not allow a prisoner-run program. Our program is not formally approved by the powers that be. My conduct and record, plus the support from the Ryans, have provided a bit of wiggle room for me to do certain things. They trust me to keep a low profile while getting high results and helping to keep the peace in this section of the prison.

Catch you soon again.

Love you muchly,
Tiyo

June 16, 2006

Pablo—

I am a bit embarrassed yet very pleased to send you the enclosed letter that was given to me by our students. As I was about to begin the class I was told, "Hold up, Tiyo, we want you to listen to what we have to say!"

Each man spoke about their new learning and appreciation of the classes and sending word to their families of becoming better men. They each shook my hand and gave me a hug. The two men I selected to take charge presented me with the enclosed letter. I was both surprised and fucked up. Yet very proud of the guys. Receiving thanks from the students is much more meaningful than from the staff. I accepted the letter on behalf of you and I. It feels good to know that you and I are making a change in the lives of some prisoners. There are app. 2,000 prisoners here. We have only 22 students, nor is our little program approved by the powers that be. The state does not want nor will it allow programs run by a prisoner for other prisoners esp. if the prisoner is a "lifer". Our little program could be shut down by certain racist staff, esp. if any of us caused trouble. Our students take care of each other and also look out for me. Helping them realize their God-given skills and talents and self-empowerment is for me pure joy. When they leave here and return to their families and begin a new positive and productive lifestyle I too will be "out there" with them in spirit. I ended my talk with them by saying, "Class dismissed, go outside and have some fun--- see you in two days!"

Thank you, Pablo---warm hugs!

We love you!
Tiyo

June 16, 2006

Dear Mr. Paul Alan Smith:

This letter is the collective views of the men who are Tiyo's students. We thank you for helping us gain a solid education and for helping Tiyo. He has often said that without your help, he could not help us. We want to demonstrate our respect for him and for you.

Tiyo is a gifted teacher and makes learning a happy and exciting experience. He teaches with a smile on his face and from his heart. He was once a very good football and baseball player. He is a hell of a jazz musician and plays the sax and the piano. He is 75 years old and could do wonderful things for people in society. He should be released. Most of us will be released. He should not be left here to die.

He always tells usthat he listens to you and takes your advice. Our request to you is to please advise him to apply for commutation or seek release through the courts. Help him get out. He should not die in prison.

Thank you.

Students of Tiyo

P.S. We are going to make him send this letter to you.

August 16, 2006

Pablo! ☺

Check this crazy story. Last Saturday the huge water main that supplies water to all areas in this prison broke. The whole system was shut down. No water to drink, no water to cook food or flush toilets. The stench was horrible. A day and a half went by before the slow-thinking powers that be finally called the local fire company and requested two fire trucks bring water to this prison. When the trucks arrived the drivers yelled, "Don't drink this water, it's polluted!"

On this cellblock we organized into three groups, e.g. one group of 8 guys to push carts carrying one large trash can to the cellblock. Group two of 8 guys would pour water from the large trash cans into the buckets the men on the cellblock would bring to the front of the cellblock and then carry back to their cells. Group three would carry buckets of water to the cells of the men who were in and not able to carry buckets of water to their cells. This process continued until app. 3 p.m. At 4 p.m. another fire truck arrived with "so-called" drinking water. We went through the same process but told the guys to boil the water with their homemade stingers. Next time I'll explain what a stinger is and how it's made. We stored enough water in trash cans etc. for the rest of the evening. Early the following day the pipe was repaired and the water turned on. Announcement was made over the PA system, "Do not drink the tap water for at least 24 hours!" I've been drinking lots of milk, eating peaches, oranges, & apples. Will continue doing so for another few days. Other guys have been drinking the water.

As of today things are back to "so-called normal". What the fuck is "normal" living in this fuckin' hell-hole? At least we're not in Darfur or some other fucked-up place. I don't know how long my old ass can withstand all this dumb shit. You help keep me alive and moving forward. Messing with you brings joy into my life.

Joe Semon told me he plans to retire within the coming 12–15 months. I hope that particular book will be published before he retires. When he leaves things will become very difficult politically. I sent word to Howard re: this matter.

Okay---enough "rap" for today. Hope you're doing okay and continuing to help people and bring peace into this world. Hang in there and stop playin' with your pee-pee!

Tiyo

DATE: September 15, 2006

TO: Paul Alan Smith

FROM: Tiyo Attallah Salah-El

RE: COST OF EDUCATION PROGRAM FOR 45 STUDENTS

       The following is the itemized budget for a nine month program. Enclosed is the current price list of items in the SCI-Dallas Commissary.

ITEM	AMOUNT		PRICE	TOTAL COST
Typewriter	1		$113.42	$113.42
Tr. Correction Tape (K Series)	3		5.40	16.20
Tr. Correction Tape (Brother)	3		5.29	14.87
Tr. Smith Corona (K Series)	3		9.85	29.55
Tr. Correction Tape (H Series)	6		5.82	34.92
Tr. Smith Ribbon (H Series)	3		8.73	26.19
Reader Lamp	2		9.43	18.86
Reader Light Bulbs	5		2.96	14.80
Extension Cord	3		1.38	4.14
Binder, 3 Ring	25		2.07	51.75
Pens, Black	45		.29	13.05
Pens, Blue	45		.29	13.05
Highlighter, Yellow	20		.44	8.80
Pencils #2	100		.11	11.00
Erasers	6		.50	3.00
Composition Book	40		1.11	44.40
Legal Pad	20		.89	17.80
Carbon Paper	100	sheets	.88	8.80
File Folder	40		1.03	41.20
Paper (Typing)	1000	sheets	3.43	34.30
TOTAL				$520.10

       At the conclusion of the program, I would like to give each student $5.00 worth of commissary items and a certificate. I did the same thing upon the completion of the Character Development classes ($5 x 45= $225) for students.
       With practical methods, we can prepare many prisoners for their GED examination and also, for those who are eligible, gain their release.
       We appreciate your financial support and strong incessant concern.

October 23, 2006

Pablo—

I waited a bit before writing regarding the major changes that have been and continue to take place at this hell-hole. A month ago new rules were posted re: the
need to make cell space for new arrivals. This prison was built to house 950 prisoners. As of today there are 2,064 prisoners, most of whom are double bunked.
The new max will be 2,100.

All prisoners who have what is listed as "A" codes, e.g. men who have exem-
plary records of behavior and meritorious achievement have been placed on the
list to be double bunked. Joe Semon informed me that my name is on the list.
During the past 2–3 weeks I've managed to help all our students who were not
already double bunked to move in with a co-student. In sum, all things considered, our guys and program continue moving forward in a positive way. The men
are hooked on learning and becoming aware of their self-empowerment. There
is an air of peace on this cellblock.

I remain in a single cage. Don't know for how long. I'll let you know
when and if it happens. Since I'm the 2nd oldest guy in this hell-hole, my
name could be next to last on the list. If the population reaches 2,100 before
my name pops up to be double bunked, I assume I'll remain in this single spi-
der hole. Just in case, I've packed up my shit because "they" (the guards) give
us one hour to move. The students will help me move should that happen. I
don't waste time or energy worrying about situations I have no control of.
What will be, will be! I have many more positive things to focus upon and
complete.

So, don't worry about me. We have a good thing going on and I'm enjoying
being a part of this historic program. Helping these men attain their GEDs and
eventual release is very special and personal to me and I hope for you too. ☺

I'll also stay in touch with both the good and not-so-good news. I'm still
working on having your phone #s approved. When I receive the "all clear" I shall
call your sorry ass. Stay tuned!!

Love you muchly,
Tee-Toe

December 27, 2006

Yo Pablo! ☺

Where are you? What are you doing? Why are you doing it? When will you secure a well-paying job?

Enclosed is a letter from the ex-superintendent Joe Ryan. He has been very ill yet strong enough to write to me. I always try hard to cheer him up by sending upbeat letters and cartoons to him. He may not be well enough to visit me this coming April. I talked with his son Bobby regarding sending the book to his dad. He suggested I do so because such would help brighten his dad's day and maybe he will open a bottle of that special wine and send a toast to us via the airwaves. I like to think Joe may have contacted the present superintendent and suggested I remain in a single cell at least for the time being until I regain my strength. I'm getting better with each new day!

Some good news! Lois Ahrens and one of her many friends, Erika Arthur, are planning to come visit me during the month of Feb. 2007. Amazing, truly amazing! They live in Northampton, MA, and plan to rent a car and drive to Dallas, PA. Erika's mom and sister live close to this prison. Their home is located on a mountain that allows them to see the lights that surround this place. I'll ask Lois and Erika to contact you and send some fotos of the visit.

On Christmas Day, I gave gifts of pound cake to each of our students. The cakes cost $1.30 ea. They were very surprised and pleased. They are doing very well. I showed pictures of you (the foto of you standing on your head received the most smiles and comments). I explained that the gifts came from you and that you send best wishes to all of them. It was the first time they received gifts at Christmas. The guys are poor. They are paid $18.00–$24.00 a month to buy a few toilet articles etc. The $100.00 you sent me was the key to the cake gifts. I hope you will not mind. It's money well spent. They will remember us when they are released.

In closing---it's a cold mofo around here! Whew! The temps remain in low 30s! The gays are saying, "It's too cold to suck a dick!"

Gotta go! Take care of your sorry ass. **HAPPY NEW YEAR!**

Your light-skin lifelong Negro friend,
Tiyo

2007
"ALL PRISONERS WILL BE FED IN THEIR CAGES"

ErikA   Tiyo   Lois
Arthur   Ahrens
              2/9/07   DALLAS, PA

Tiyo with his friend Lois Ahrens (right), founding director of Real Cost of Prisons
Project, who introduced Tiyo to a number of his other dedicated correspondents,
including Erika Arthur (left).

February 19, 2007

Yo Pablo! ☺

There has been so much fuckin' snow that this hell-hole was 80 percent shut down! Plus the temps have been and continue to be app. 3–4 degrees! Eek! Hell of a way to live. Don't you dare tell me how hot & sunny Calif. is! Fuck you! ☺

The waiting list re: guys wanting to become part of our education program continues to expand. I've got to figure out how to schedule 107 guys for 5-day-a-week classes. The guards love it because they know things will be handled without any trouble which makes their job a lot easier. This week I'll know the results of who passed the Pre-GED test and will relay the news to you. No doubt some of the guys will have to take the test again. But we will keep trying to get as close to 100 percent as possible. I'm planning a graduation day for the guys, e.g. giving certificates and chips, cookies, candy, and lots of teasing & risque jokes. By the way, we have developed 12, yes 12, new leaders who can take over our program with teaching and inspiring the students. Such will allow me to sort of float between each class and see how things are going. Should anything happen to me the program will continue. I try to plan ahead. I wish we could send 500–600 guys to the Pre-GED test and on to the GED and next help them gain parole. There are 2,084 prisoners here. I want to help half of them attain release.

Hope you are busy and doing okay, plus having a bit of fun. Remember, "All work and no play makes Jake jerk off!" ☺

Take care of your sorry ass. I'll always stay in touch.

Love you muchly!
Tiyo

March 26, 2007

Hi Pablo—

Gotta share the enclosed note with you and explain the "why". Almost on a daily diet I receive oral and written requests for all sorts of things esp. re: education and legal situations. This is the first time one of my top crew members (who is tutoring 15 of our students) requested my advice. He is white and the students are all black. It's his first time in front of a class of poor inner-city blacks. I choose him to teach the class because it would be a great learning experience for him and the students. I rotate the tutors so that they and the students keep things fresh, upbeat and positive. I think he may have not considered how the students think about him as a tutor/talker. It's going to be interesting to see how this plays out. Lots of K-razy shit happens here! This man (white) had very little experience with blacks & Hispanics while he was growing up etc., e.g. middle-class gringo. ☺ First time in prison—good education and leadership skills and talent, enjoys teaching and helping others. That is why I selected him to tutor blacks & Hispanics. I'm confident in the offing he will find ways to adjust, improve and understand people of color. I want to not only help prisoners gain GEDs but also to develop more leaders/instructors/teachers and also help them attain release. If they take a small bit of me with them when they leave this hell-hole, (and many of them leave), I'll be "free" also, viz. my spirit will be "out there"—my physical body will still be here. That's my crazy-ass plan to finally be released from prison.

    Why am I writing such crazy shit to your sorry ass? You're fucked up in the head more than me! Enough of this for now. Hope you're feeling better with each new day. Get laid soon via that female! Eek! ☺

Later,
Tiyo

April 20, 2007

Hi Ho Amigo!

Welcome home!! Hope you had a fine time in China. Today I decided to relax a bit from the pressures of our program and "talk" with you about a funding plan I've been working on for our education program. I assume upon your return you'll be super busy with the many tasks and responsibilities you have. That possibility moves me to cut to the chase. Fasten your safety belt!

A month ago in one of your letters you posed the question "have I asked other folks to help fund the program?" My response at that time was "no". Later on I spent a lot of time thinking about your question and began thinking of ways to create and execute a plan that would bring about a workable and acceptable response and solution and bring it into play. Such is the impetus for this letter.

My goal during the past years has been to connect with as many prisoners as possible to let them know that we all have the power to make changes in our lives that can help us live with better health, more joy, common sense and inner peace. My intention is to teach prisoners what I have learned to do for myself. I encourage students to be conscious of what they are doing in the moment. So much of stress and anxiety in prison is about focusing on what could go wrong or what we don't have control over. I often tell the guys to think about what we have to be grateful for, and compare what people are dealing with on a daily basis in Darfur, Iraq, Afghanistan and elsewhere.

I want them to look at certain events of life as part of their path in life and part of their learning growth. Hopefully, they will then recognize challenges not as threats but as opportunities to use their new learning, skills and talents. The time has arrived for us to set new goals and priorities. My plan is an opportunity for us to exercise our capacity for discovering more of what we are able to achieve. This plan can be viewed as an occasion that calls on us to live up to our full creative potential. I want the program to generate our own funding and become self-sustaining without asking you or anyone on the outside to send us money. I've discussed the following with all involved with the program and gave them two weeks to think about it and discuss it among themselves.

I am fully aware that most of the students receive $15–$18 per month and most of that money is spent on basic toilet articles. I asked them to consider spending $1.00 to purchase a few pens, pencils and some paper from the commissary. Those who can and are willing to donate $5.00 will be asked to buy tablets, carbon paper and extra pens, pencils and typing paper. I have taken the job of cleaning the shower room seven days a week and will buy the extra typewriters and all extra supplies. I am paid $28.00 per month. This plan can become an interesting lesson in learning the management of our money and achieving a feeling of personal and collective pride. The students and my friends and supporters know of my self-determination and self-empowerment. I give to all whom I interact with the gift of myself, my appreciation, attention, individuality and friendship. Together we will rise to new heights of understanding and achievement. The positiveness we all apply in our everyday living brings about beneficial results.

You have carried us for a long time and allowed us to gain our sea legs. You have helped most of the students to take and pass the GED test. Some have gained their GEDs and made parole. We must now take full charge and swim or sink on our own merit & sweat. I ask that you allow me to carry this program forward on my own. I need and willing accept this challenge. Do not send me more money. I am confident that in time you will become more proud of us. We are going to be okay. I'll keep you posted.

Again, welcome home amigo! Warm hugs and lifelong love.

Who knows, one day colored people could take over the world!!

TEEEEEEEEEEEEOOOOOOOOOOH!

May 9, 2007

Que pasa, my ever-lovin' lifelong amigo! ☺

Today has been extra special! Ex-superintendent Joe Ryan came to visit me! His son Bobby (who is the supervisor of the laundry) called (via his cell phone) this cellblock and asked the block guard to give me a pass and to come to the laundry. When I arrived his dad was there. Joe and I hugged for a long time. Then we began laughing and teasing. His son suggested his dad and I go into the office to talk. Joe and I talked for a long time. We covered a range of topics. He spoke of his stroke. He now walks with a cane; he showed me his hands that are arthritic, fingers curled, problem with arms, hips and legs. He is 78 years old. I'll be 75 years old this coming Sept. 13th. He said he was determined to come visit me. We spoke about you and the <u>special</u> <u>gift</u> ☺ you sent him. He again expressed his surprise and appreciation. When we departed the office I was "allowed" to slowly walk with him to the main front gate. The guards in the towers called out to us, "Hey, Joe, take Tiyo out with you. We won't shoot him!" It was the first time I was allowed to walk to the main gate. When the gate opened, Joe & I hugged and he said, "If you need me, write a letter; I'll always help you. I've heard of the good work you are doing. It's time for you to focus on your own needs. I don't have much money on me but I'm going to leave half of it to you!" This is a truly historic event. Never before has a superintendent returned not only to visit a prisoner but to give money. When I returned to this cage, the block handed me the enclosed cash slip. For me, it's not the amount that is important, it's his visit and his gesture of kindness that touched deep into the marrow of bones and into my soul.

<u>Then</u> <u>came</u> <u>another</u> <u>surprise</u>! The same guard returned and said, "Tiyo, who do you know in China?" He then handed me your card! Wow! ☺ Man, I did a little dance of happiness! <u>Thank you very much</u>! To receive your card and to have a visit with Joe have made this a very special day for me. You guys are very special to me and inspire me to reach for higher goals and <u>never ever give up</u>!

I've been incarcerated for over 30 years; have had some ups & downs, have been called a nigger by a staff member; but did not lose my self-control; kept on moving forward with my positive mission, have hung tough when dealing with my medical & health problems etc. Days like today make me feel proud of myself. Having you and Howard publish my book, and you funding our education program, plus your cards, letters and the great teasing you and I do, keeps me alive and keepin' on! I am forever beholden to you for the zillion special favors and support you bestow upon me. If you could cook I'd marry your sorry ass! ☺

> Warm hugs, and incessant love and respect,
> Tiyo

WELCOME HOME! ☺

September 11, 2007

Hi Pablo—

Different type letter to send to you. Today this hell-hole is "lockdown". All prisoners will be fed in their cages. Last time during the "lockdown" our program took a huge hit. I promised you such would not again catch me off guard. All is cool regarding our supplies and students. We shall begin classes tomorrow.

There is a much more important matter to relay to you. I received a wonderful letter from Howard Zinn informing me that he and Roz understand, respect and support my decision not to apply for commutation. What knocked me off balance was when he explained that my decision strangely resembles the decision Roz recently made in her own situation, e.g. in July she went through a series of medical tests resulting in a diagnosis of ovarian cancer. This is not curable but it can be put off for some years by surgery and chemotherapy. Roz does not want to go through six months of that in order to prolong her life by a few years. She wants to live out her remaining time (and no one can predict what that means) in peace. She feels good about her life so far and wants to be in control of the rest of it rather than be subject to someone else's decisions. For me, she continues to maintain her spirit with great courage and is moving valiantly into each day. I shall cheer her on via cards, letters and a couple surprise happy phone calls. I'm confident you'll do much the same for them and even better than my love and support. Thank you. I shall write a happy letter to both of them. Hope you are doing okay. I am easy.

Tiyo

* Extra soulful thanks for the very hip birthday card. With all due respect and appreciation, you need to take a crash course in drawing. ☺ You make me smile whenever I need it most.

9-11-07

Hi Pablo—

Different type letter to send to you. Today this hell-hole is "Lock-down". All prisoners will be fed in their cages. Last time during the "lock-down" our program took a huge hit. I promised you such would not again catch me off guard. All is cool regarding our supplies and students. We shall begin classes tomorrow.

There is a much more important matter to relay to you. I received a wonderful letter from Howard Zinn informing me that he and Roz understands, respects and supports my decision not to apply for commutation. What knocked me off balance was when he explained that my decision strangely resembles the decision Roz recently made in her own situation, e.g. she went through a series of medical tests resulting in a diagnosis of ovarian cancer. This is not curable but it can be put off for some years by surgery and chemotherapy. Roz does not want to go through six months of that in order to prolong her life by a few years. She wants to live out her remaining time (and no one can predict what that means) in peace. She feels good about her life so far and wants to be in control of the rest of it rather than be subject to someone else's decisions. For me, she continues to maintain her spirit with great courage and is moving valiantly into each day. I shall cheer her on via cards, letters and a couple surprise happy phone calls. I'm confident you'll do much the same for them and even better than my love and support. Thank you. I shall write a happy letter to both of them. Hope you are doing okay. I am easy.

Tato

✱ Extra soulful thanks for the very hip birthday card. With all due respect and appreciation, you need to take a crash course in drawing. ☺ You make me smile whenever I need it most.

November 22, 2007

Pablo—

Today (Thanksgiving) guess what happened? The lights, heat and water were turned off and the prison has been on lockdown. This place is slowly falling apart. The 2nd shift guards had to pass out a brown bag with one small apple, 2 thin slices of cheese & a stale taco shell to 2,082 prisoners who were yellin' & cussin'. Whew! By 5:30 p.m. it was pitch-black on each cellblock and inside the cages. Guards used flashlights to walk around and count bodies. No showers tonight. I hope the lockdown will be over tomorrow. I've got to check on our students.

For now I'm going to try to go to sleep. I need to regroup my plans for the coming days. Don't ever be sent to prison. It's pure fucking hell.

Tiyo

*Fuck G. W. Bush! ☺

December 18, 2007

Yo Pablo!

Enclosed is a copy of the results of our students who took the GED exam. All things considered they did very well and I'm proud of them. They hung tough during some stressful times at this hell-hole. The 6 who failed missed by 4–6 points. They can retake the test in 6 months. I'll talk with the powers that be in the school re: a possible way and time for our one student who did not take the exam due to the death of his sister. I'm keeping close watch on him. I don't want him to be released from here with thoughts of tracking down and doing harm to the person who killed his sister.

Later on I'll explain in detail why I'm taking a 4–6 week break. I'm scheduled to see the doctor the 1st or 2nd week of Jan. My lower back, hips, legs and feet are in need of serious attention and repair. It's difficult for me to walk. I'm bent over slightly and limping a lot. Old age is a bitch! ☺ I'll be in touch soon. Behave yourself and get a fuckin' job! ☺

Tiyo

December 18, 2007

TO: Monty Neill, Howard Zinn, Paul Alan Smith, Lois Ahrens,
Erika Arthur, Mecke Nagel, Elizabeth Dede, Carrie Dearborn,
Marina Drummer, Bev and Wally Williams.

RE: GED test results of each of our 75 students.
        (2,000 points needed to pass)

2,007	2,064	2,816
2,009	2,075	2,837
2,011	2,079	2,849
2,012	2,084	2,872
2,014	2,094	2,874
2,018	2,097	2,878
2,020	2,128	2,882
2,021	2,141	2,884
2,022	2,159	2,885
2,024	2,278	2,887
2,026	2,297	2,889
2,027	2,340	2,893
2,028	2,374	2,895
2,029	2,389	2,896
2,030	2,431	2,897
2,034	2,486	2,899
2,037	2,497	2,908
2,038	2,515	2,927
2,039	2,538	
2,041	2,648	
2,044	2,687	
2,046	2,698	
2,049	2,718	
2,051	2,767	
2,062	2,789	

A total of 68 Students passed the test.
Six students failed the test.

Due to tragic situation that happened to the sister
of one of our students he did not take the test. I will
try to find a way for him to take test at a later date.

I plan to take a 4-6 week break to rest a bit. I will
restart the program the first or second week of February.
Next year I plan to help 100 prisoners gain a GED. I plan
to keep doing this program for many more years. Stay tuned!

                Love you all muchly!

December 31, 2007

Yo Pablo! ☺

I just talked with Superintendent Wynder. He informed me he received a copy of my book. He thanked me for the gift. ☺ He retires January 11th, 2008. It was nice for him to come to this particular cellblock today and talk with me. Thank you very much! You continue bringing much joy into my life.

I hope you are feeling better with each new day. I always speak your name when I pray. I also include your mom, dad, sister and brother. I hope you get well soon so that I can start teasing you again.

Tiyo

2008
"I'M TRYING TO DEVELOP LEADERS"

January 17, 2008

Pablo!

It's been over 30 years since I've ate such meats. Eek! Check out enclosed. Our lifelong loving friend stays super busy. Lois Ahrens sent the article to me.

Hope you got the hip healing feeling. I'm coming along slowly. The shots in my hips are incredibly miserable and painful. Whew! I'm walking a bit better. The guys are bringing me sandwiches, fruit, milk, soup, etc. They take turns cleaning the shower room for me. The doctor gave me Clonidine Hcl for my B/P and Diltiazem 300 mg for my B/P, Vitamin B-Complex, Furosemide, Levothyroxine, Aspirin-low 81 mg, Lovastatin, plus Prednisone for my arthritis and Elavil. Am I fucked up or what? ☺ The doctor informed me that I will have pain until I die. Hell of a thing for him to say. But what the fuck. Such is life. I want and need to get back on my feet in order to prepare for our program.

The new warden, Michael Klopotoski, is now in charge and is putting into place a bunch of new oppressive rules. He is a control freak. Due to the escape of a lifer from another prison, Klopotoski has stopped not just "lifers" from moving around inside this hell-hole but <u>all</u> prisoners. Cells are searched every 4 days. I will draw up a memo for our students re: our program and how to deal with the extra stress etc. I'll send you a copy. We will have to navigate around the new rules. I've received requests from <u>102</u> prisoners who want to participate in our program. I'll keep you posted as we move forward.

I think it best that we not worry Howard about my health problems. He has lots of other things to take care of. Anyway, I'll be okay in another couple of weeks. I want to start our program on the 1st or 2nd week of Feb.

Take care of yourself and <u>get well soon</u>! I need to <u>tease you</u> so that I can <u>get on my feet</u>!

Later,
Tiyo

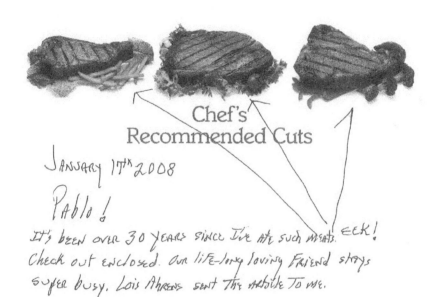

Chef's
Recommended Cuts

January 17th 2008

Pablo!

It's been over 30 years since I've ate such meats. EEK!
Check out enclosed. Our life-long loving friend stays
super busy. Lois Ahrens sent the article to me.

Hope you got the hip healing feeling. I'm coming along
slowly. The shots in my hips are incredibly miserable and
painful. Whew! I'm walking a bit better. The guys are bringing me
sandwiches, fruit, milk, soup, etc. they take turns cleaning the shower
room for me. The doctor gave me Clonidine Hcl for my B/P and
Diltiazem 300mg for my B/P, Vitamin B-Complex, Furosemide, Levothyroxine
Aspir-low 81mg, Lovastatin, plus prednisone for my arthritis and Elavil.
Am I fucked up or what? 😊

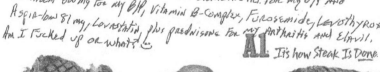

A1 It's how Steak Is Done.

SP3-184

The doctor informed me that I will have pain until I die. Hell of a thing for him to say. But what the fuck. Such is life. I want and need to get back on my feet in order to prepare for our program. The new warden, Michael Klopotoski is now in charge and is putting into place a bunch of new oppressive rules. He is a control freak. Due to the escape of a lifer from another prison, Klopotoski has stopped not just "lifers" from moving around inside this hell-hole, but ALL prisoners. Cells are searched every 4 days. I will draw up a memo for our students, RE: our program and how to deal with the extra stress, etc. I'll send you a copy. We will have to navigate around the new rules. I've received requests from 102 prisoners who want to participate in our program. I'll keep you posted as we move forward.

I think it best that we not worry Howard about my health problems. He has lots of other things to take care of. Anyway, I'll be okay in another couple of weeks. I want to start our program the 1st or 2nd week of Feb.

Take care of yourself and get well soon! I need to tease you so that I can get on my feet! Later,
Tiyo

January 20, 2008

TO. New Students

RE: Special GED Program

FROM:Tiyo Attallah Salah-EL

Introduction.

Three years ago this program was created to help prisoners
gain a GED. Most prisoners are required to obtain a GED in
order to be eligible for Pre-Release/Half-Way House
programs. This program is based upon self-direction, self-
determination and self-empowerment. In many ways you will
control your progress. This program takes about six to nine
months to complete.

A Tutor, who has attained a GED will be assigned to help you
throughout the program. The GED exam is given in the school
building under the supervision of the school Administrator.
A notice as to the day and time of the exam will be posted
ON each cell block. You must score 2,000 or more points to
pass the exam. You will be supplied with the necessary
supplies at no cost to you. Funding for this program is
provided by the well-known Historian, Howard Zinn and Paul
Alan Smith, a top Hollywood Agent. Lois Ahrens, the
Director of the Real Cost of Prisons Project, created and
provides special certificates that will be given to each
student upon completion of the program.

Please remember that we are in prison. You must prepare
mentally to deal with disruptions such as lock-downs, cell
and body searches and destruction of your papers by guards.
If caught with drugs or wine the guards will put you in "the
Hole". Please maintain your composure. Focus on your
studies, personal dignity, your family and loved ones and
most importantly your freedom from this prison.

Due to the new rules that are now in place we cannot move
around like we use to. However, should you want to talk
with me ask your Tutor to relay word to me. I will make
arrangements to meet you in the yard or gym.

                Best of luck to each of you.

cc: Howard Zinn
    Paul Alan Smith
    Lois Ahrens
    File(1)

Feb 10, 2008

Dear Tiyo —
I am so honored
that you have named
me, as well as Paul Alan
Smith, as sponsor of the
Certificate of Achievement for
your 102 students!

What an accomplishment
for you to have a profound
effect on the lives of 102 human
beings. We are all proud of
you and what you are
doing.
                    Love —
                    Howard &
                    Roz

PS Money order will be enclosed

February 11, 2008

Pablo!

Your timing is fuckin X-cellent! First off, thank you for the bread! It arrived today, the very day our 102 students began studying for their GEDs. We started on a positive note. I think they'll do okay. I will check on them each week to help resolve any problems etc. The majority are young, e.g. 21 to 26–27 years old. A lot of them call me "Mr. Tiyo". They are trying to show respect. I suggested they call me Tiyo. Second issue to bring to your sorry-ass attention is "de" fact that today I received yet another wonderful ♥ gift package ♥ of fotos re: your travels to Nayarit y Jalisco, MX. Wow! You are something else! Check this out. Both shifts of guards on this cellblock have asked me to share the pictures with them. They make phone calls to other guards on other cellblocks to "come see the wonderful pictures from Tiyo's friend who lives in Beverly Hills, CA, and is a Hollywood agent!" Do you realize that most of the guards and staff members, plus all the prisoners, including me, have not been to any of the places in the world that you have traveled to? News has spread that "Tiyo has lots of special pictures!" No one has ever received such a huge amount of pictures that have arrived at this prison—only happened to old man Tiyo! ☺ The doctor and RNs want to see the pictures. I plan to take one package of flicks to them once a week. You have given me a huge amount of positive PR. Thank you!! ☺

Finally—today, Joe Semon talked with me for a long time re: commutation, e.g. my conduct, education, age, the support I would receive from all staff members, etc. I listened and did not mentioned the decision I made months ago when Lois Ahrens came to visit and she and I discussed the commutation situation. I've not changed my mind. I'm at peace with myself and my decision. I deeply appreciate the strong support you, Howard, Lois and others gave regarding my decision. I also appreciate people such as Semon, Joe Ryan, et al. wanting me to be released. I'm focused on our education program. I need this project to help me stay active, and positive and productive. I've found a new purpose in life. I enjoy helping these guys and at the same time learning a new way of life for myself. I don't want you to worry about me. I shall keep going until I die. I also want to show the deep love and respect I have for you & Howard. I want to give back something positive to you guys for giving me so very much to live and die for. I hope you'll understand where I'm coming from. It's deep and it's for real.

♥ Tiyo

February 20, 2008

Pablo, Pablo, Crazy-Ass Pablo! ☺

Yesterday I received 167 fotos of "Dougie Does Thailand". I received word that the folks in the mailroom are enjoying looking at the pictures and are wondering, "Who is the person sending these pictures to Tiyo?" Since I'm not a snitch I'll not give you up to "de" po-lice!

Some of your students have asked, "Yo, Tiyo, why don't you ask your friend to become the warden at this prison?" That would really be fucked up! Eek! Some good has come of all this attention re: the pictures, e.g. I've not been stripped searched, nor cell searched, nor my books, papers, thrashed. There has been a lot of guards visiting me requesting to see the pictures. Somethings just seem to happen at the right time and place, yes, even in a prison setting. Who would have "tunk it" that such great gifts would make history at this place, esp. this hell-hole. More people now know "Tiyo" than ever before. Maybe someone will take me home with them! Eek! ☺

We are into the 2nd week of our education program. So far, things are going well and it appears the students are enjoying a new way to spend their time instead of milling around and bored day after day, wasting their lives. It's a shame that the state will not provide meaningful programs for all 2,086 prisoners. What a fuckin' waste of human life. Prisons are multi-billion-dollar businesses wasting taxpayers' money! When will the public wake the fuck up?

Gotta go! Send more flicks! ☺ I love it! ☺

♥ Tiyo

P.S. I love the pictures of you diving and doing a flip into the sea! Wow! ☺ I placed pictures of you on the walls of this cage. I "talk to you" everyday!

March 2, 2008

Hello Pablo! ☺

Enclosed are letters from Howard Zinn, Joe Ryan and Erika Arthur. Interesting news from them. I thought it best that you become aware of their words, plus, I save a bit of time writing a long letter to you. Eek! ☺

Our program is moving along very well. I am receiving requests from not just short-time prisoners but, at long last, lifers! I've been trying for app. 2 years to motivate "some" lifers to become involved with education, music, art, pen pals, etc. instead of sitting around playing cards or watching TV 12–14 hours a day. There are over 453 lifers here at SCI-Dallas. The majority have given up on life and their lives. It's sad and tragic. I try to set a positive example by not just talking about getting involved with positive activities but doing it, producing it right before their eyes, and having a bit of fun doing it! ☺ Last week seven lifers came to this cage and said, "Tiyo, we want to try to get a GED and want you to sign us up!" I almost wet myself! ☺ I didn't want them to wait until next year, so old pussy me offered to start them this week. Since they are older men, 55–62 years of age, I'll be their tutor. Plus, it's best because I'm a lifer too. I hope you'll understand my decision. One day, someone will take my place. I'm trying to develop leaders. Enough "rap" for now.

Hope you are okay and back at work. I still want to buy your home. My first offer is $25.95. Take it under consideration. ☺

❤ Tiyo

March 10, 2008

Yo Mofo Pablo! ☺

Brief update re: possible interview with Erika Arthur. If the new superintendent says "no" I have a "plan B". ☺ E.g. I'll do it via the phones. I'll keep you posted.

The weather here is really bad, e.g. lots of snow, rain and cold, really cold weather. Prisoners are not allowed to go to the yard when the temps drop below 32 degrees. The temps for the past week and a half have been 4 degrees below reaching a high (??) of 27 degrees! Not allowing these thugs to go to the yard creates more stress and tensions between prisoners & guards and prisoners & prisoners. For example, last week a fight took place between two prisoners (both big & black). The guy who lost the fight waited two days before going up to the 2nd range with his TV and waited for the winner of the fight (who was downstairs walking to the front of this cellblock), threw the TV, hitting the winner in the head, and then threws a tub of boiling water on the guy. Blood and hot water flowed from the victim. Guards came running with clubs, and locked us all down. It was crazy. The guards picked the guy up and carried him to the hospital while other guards rushed upstairs to cuff and escort the "loser" to "the Hole". Never a dull day here. I'm glad our students were not involved. I try to keep our students busy with positive projects. No time to lay around and get into trouble.

Hope you are back at work. I've decided not to buy your house. It's too small!! ☺

Love you muchly,
Tiyo

April 4, 2008

Pablo! ☺

Yesterday at app. 4:10 p.m., I was returned to and placed in the prison hospital. I'm still in the prison hospital. Not feeling my best but still hangin' tough. Lots of crazy news to send your way but first allow me to express my deep love, respect and appreciation for going beyond medal of lifelong friendship and calling me from Peru and allowing me to know you were thinking about me as I lay on my back in the hospital bed. Tears flowed uncontrolled from my eyes as my body was shaking. Man, I was fucked up with pure joy. Never in my life have I ever experienced such emotions. You are truly an amazing person and my wonderful loving friend!

Allow me to give a brief update re: my condition. After 75 years of life I've been informed that I have diabetes. Last week my sugar was 571! Whew! At first, "they" assumed I was having a heart attack. Semon called the guards & the hospital (he also walked to the hospital and made sure I was covered and placed in the ambulance). The folks at the outside hospital provided excellent treatment, e.g. two CAT scans, B/P tests, sugar tests, tasty food (after 4 days of fasting), sugar is down to 120–125 levels. Received visits with Erika Arthur, Mecke Nagel (Erika bought a bunch of flowers), received phone calls from Monty Neill & Lois Ahrens. 12 guards from SCI-Dallas stopped by to check on & cheer me on—then entered the one and only Joe Ryan! I almost wet myself! He and I talked & teased for app. 45 min. It was a really good visit and a toe-tappin' soulful surprise. The next day Superintendent Wynder sent greetings to me.

Now for a bit of business re: our education program. When news was spread that I left the prison and was taken to the outside hospital, I'm sorry to report that the tutors panicked and stopped teaching. I blame myself for not having in place a plan B. Whenever I'm released from the prison hospital I'll regroup and create a fall back plan. I will meet with all involved and explain the importance of keeping the program moving forward regardless of what could happen to me.

Before becoming ill I had begun to discuss with Lois, Erika, and a few others that we must soon find someone to take my place, hopefully it would be someone "out there". I've been searching for the right type in-house prisoner, e.g. one or two of our current tutors. However, our tutors will soon be placed in the pre-release halfway house and drug programs. What we need are "long tim-ers" who have come to grips with their situations, e.g. dying in prison, yet can dig down deep within themselves and say "fuck it" I'll go out helping others get out.

Then comes the issues of trust and respect of not only the students, guards, prison staff but of you, Zinn, Lois, Erika, and of course me. It will be and is a daunting task. I hope you, Zinn, Lois, Erika, et al. will discuss these issues and later let me know your thoughts. I'll do all I can from in here. Okay!

Tiyo with his good friend and correspondent Professor Mecke Nagel at SCI Dallas.

May 28, 2008

Dear Paul,

Today, I received word from Lois Ahrens re: the passing of Roz. The people in the SCI-Dallas held her letter for 7 days before sending it to me. The news was really slow reaching me. Thank you for contacting Lois Ahrens. I will write a letter of love, respect and lifelong support to Howard. I'm not good dealing with these type situations.

Due to my "snail mail" taking more time to reach Howard will you send him a brief email stating that a letter from me is on its way to him? At this present time my head is messed up. Yes, I know I'm leaning on you. Sometimes life is not fair.

Thanks!
Tiyo

August 4, 2008

Pablo!

No doubt some of my words to you today will be profoundly emotional and truthful. I have to explain some things; some personal things.

You have asked me why I cry at times of seeing and talking with you, e.g. during the phone call regarding the death of my sister Bette and during your recent visit and times when I'm alone in this cage. What brought this "confession" on is the wonderful letter I just received from our lifelong loving friend Howard Zinn. He informed me how happy he was upon receiving the pictures of you and me in the visiting room and that he wants me to take better care of myself and that he loves you and me very much and that we are both needed. It is Howard who introduced us to each other. I'm super proud and happy to know that you and I can bring some joy into his life esp. now that Roz has passed. Being able to bring joy into his life (esp. from this prison cage) is special, very special to me. You can do many more amazing things for him than I could ever dream of doing. I willing give my life for you guys. That is why I work my ass off helping some prisoners gain a GED and hopefully release from this hell-hole. Ever since we met my life has become more interesting and yes, more fun, esp. teasing you.

In app. 60 days our program for 2008 will come to a close. I have informed most of our current and future wannabes that I will not take on another group during 2009. Such a decision has brought about a degree of anger for some and offers of bags of reefer, extra special foods, visits from white, black and Latino women and money if I continue the program. I have refused all such bullshit offers. I have explained that I plan to focus upon creating a GED handbook that hopefully will be made available to the 2.3 million prisoners in America. Plus, I explained (not in specific detail) the situation regarding my health. Most prisoners, staff and guards, and hospital staff are aware that I'm no longer 100 percent healthy. I'm not able to take on 100 students. The handbook will be my final project. I want to rest, read, listen to music, sort of "smell the roses" during my last years on this planet. I also would like to help you with your "wonderful dream project". Gimme a job! ☺

Check out the enclosed materials! Mecke did a great job with my paper and spreading my name during the ICOPA affair in London. Who would have "tunk it" that folks from various parts of the world would be interested in my work. Thank you for helping me write a good paper.

Finally, allow me to close with why you've witnessed me cry when I talk with you, and when I see you and when I talk to and touch your pictures. I have never in my life done that with any other human being, not even my sister Bette. My tears are tears of love, respect and joy, and best of all tears of lifelong friendship. I have learned a lot from you and Howard and you guys help me to "keep on keepin' on"! I thank you for being my lifelong friend

Catch you soon again,
♥ Tiyo

P.S. Joe Semon has left. If for any reason you call here re: me please ask for a Mr. Keller. The person who now replaced Semon is a Red Neck Racist. He is not well-liked by prisoners nor many staff members. Be careful if you ever talk with him.

2009
"I REFUSE TO TAKE CHEMO"

January 19, 2009, MLK Holiday

Hi Pablo—

"Gotta" relay some info your way. I'm chippin' away at our GED project, e.g. bought lots of paper, pens, large tablets, typing ribbons, carbon paper, etc. I will handwrite all six sections then try to do as much typing as my hands/fingers will allow. The arthritis is slowly doing a job on my legs, hips, back and hands. I'm hangin' tough as best I can. The extra 22 steel bunks have arrived on this cellblock. The workers, viz. the prisoners, will do all the work, e.g. drilling, hammering, lifting, etc. There will be a lot of noise, yelling, cussing, etc. After they complete their work the counselors will tell the guards to inform which prisoners are to double up. I'm becoming better prepared mentally when they come for me. In a strange fucked-up way the GED handbook has filled a void that existed in my mind. I needed a hard, positive project to work on instead of wasting my time and energy worrying about a situation I had no control over. So be it! Fuck 'em! I assume it will take me much longer to complete the handbook, esp. when there is another person in the cell with me.

I've also decided to take things one day at a time. My health-related issues are much more difficult than I first realized. That's another reason why I want to push hard and complete the project as soon as possible. This may well be my last project. I don't think I have much gas left in my tank for many more years on this planet. I have all the materials needed to get the job done. I'll keep you posted as things come together. By the way, it's fuckin' freeeezing in this area, e.g. 4°–7°, with snow piled up everywhere. Also, I relayed news that you sent me some bread for boots, long johns, socks, etc. I received a beautiful card from H. Zinn. Last week I had a groovy visit with Mecke Nagel. Finally, tomorrow a Negro will become the 44th president of the U.S. of America. Truly amazing and historic! I love it! Glad I'm still alive to witness some very hip political shit hap'nin'! ☺

Take care of yourself and smoke a joint or three for me. ☺

Love you muchly,
Tiyo

Real Cost of Prisons Project
Lois Ahrens
Director
5 Warfield Place
Northampton, MA 01060

February 24, 2009

Dear Tiyo,

First, you will be getting, I hope soon, a copy of what Aaron Rubinstein has put up on UMass Special Collections website. I couldn't print all out on my computer, so I asked him to do it and he willingly agreed. CONGRATULATIONS! This is such a major and important contribution to anyone, anywhere around the world, who wants to do research. I am not sure if it has ever been done before. It was very, very good that Aaron did all of the work cataloging your materials and writing the finding, etc. but this really brings it to a world-wide audience. Really it does. I am so happy about it and I know you will be too! Because you understand the major need for this kind of information if people are to even begin to understand the impact of caging someone for life!

Anyhow, I am so pleased that your collection is now out there in cyberspace for millions to read and know about. Aaron has sent out an announcement to everyone about it and I have sent out an additional announcement to prison activists/abolitionists in PA and around the country. It is a wonderful achievement.

Lois

3-3-09

$3\sqrt[3]{9}$ ☺

Pablo!
This is indeed some happy News to send you. Who would have Tunk it could happen to an old colored guy like me? eek! You and Zinn are in my heart, soul and collection at The W.E.B. DuBois Library at U. Mass. Thank you muchly for helping me to make a bit of positive history. I love you muchly!
Tiyo

May 10, 2009

Hi Pablo!

Some brief but good news to send to you. Last Thursday, May 7th, Joe Ryan came to see and talk with me and with the new superintendent, regarding the issue of double bunking or not double bunking a "particular prisoner" plus other issues. I was not present at the meeting between Ryan and the new powers that be but later on he and I met and had a great time talking, teasing, laughing, and having our pictures taken. I received word that I will not be double bunked.

It was your gesture of support of me that touched Ryan in many positive ways. He stays in touch with me via the mails. He has had two strokes and his left knee is numb and stiff due to arthritis. The fingers on his hands are curled into a fist due to arthritis. He is 81 years old. He and I have known each other for over 30 years. He is a very nice man. I respect him. It is indeed rare for a prisoner to have a super special relationship with the warden that will no doubt continue until he and I depart this world.

I want you to reflect upon your inner goodness and kindness towards others. You have helped lots and lots of people in America and various parts of the world; people who are young, old, white, black, yellow, brown, rich, poor, middle and upper-middle class, gay, straight, bisexual and of course an old life-sentenced prisoner. You even made a once in a lifetime historic trip to Dallas Prison to visit this old-ass prisoner. It was a wonderful visit with you. Meeting you in person (esp. before I die) was very important to me. Years ago Howard Zinn visited me. That too was great and special. You and Howard are remarkable men. I'm really pleased that Howard introduced you to me and me to you. ☺

Finally, you have taken excellent care of me in many special ways. You have brought much joy and new learning into my life, e.g. letters, cards, money, beautiful pictures from various parts of the world, and your continued strong and incessant support. Thank you for reaching back and helping me and others. I am honored to know you and to have earned your friendship. You are a very important part of my life. I'm forever beholden to you.

Best wishes!
Tiyo

August 14, 2009

Pablo—

This will no doubt be a short fucked-up letter. I'll cut to the chase then give a very brief explanation. Here is the crappy news. I have prostate cancer. Please don't pity me nor feel sorry, etc. What will be will be. This coming Sept. 13th I'll be 77. I refuse to take chemo. By the time "it" takes its toll on me I hope to be at least 90 years old. Eek!

Erika Arthur came to visit me on Monday, Oct. 10th, and I discussed my medical situation with her. Our talk went well and I decided to relay this fucked-up news to you, Zinn, Mecke, Monty Neill and Lois. I'd rather not have long discussions about it.

I hope you'll not mind too much if I continue writing and mailing crazy-ass letters and cards to you. I wanna stay as happy as long as I can. I'm almost finished writing the GED handbook for thugs. Erika is doing all the typing etc. She plans to email you a copy of what I've done so far. Please remember it's a 1st draft, not the final draft. Please send feedback and feed forward.

Finally, just want to thank you for your solid and inspiring friendship. I gotta give Howard Zinn huge, groovy credit for bringing you into my fucked-up life. Enough of this rap for now. I'll be in touch soon again. Hang in there my friend.

♥ Tiyo

September 5, 2009

Dear Tiyo:

  Thank you for your recent letter. It is always good to hear from you,
even when you are telling about your various ailments. I have a list
myself: loss of hearing, poor vision, can't walk far, can't stand long.

But like you, I am looking at the positive side of things. You are good
model for me, because after all, your situation is a lot more repressive
than mine, and yet you maintain a wonderful spirit. So many people can
learn from that.

When I hear you say that you don't know how much longer you will be
on this earth, I understand. I just turned 87, and I feel I don't have much
to go. But I don't feel bad about it. Since Roz died, I have been
philosophical, as she was, and as you are, about coming to the end,
because the important thing is that you have lived a good life. In your
case, you have done amazing things from the confines of your
imprisonment. You have organized a movement for the abolition of
prisons, you have had your ideas spread across the nation and across the
globe. You had contributed to the education of your fellow prisoners in a
very practical way. You have inspired countless people by your
example of what one person can do against enormous odds. So when
you leave this earth you know you will have contributed to the moral
development of future generations. And you have made so many good
friends, who are devoted to you and love you. That is a legacy that very
few people, whatever prestige and wealth they have accumulated, can
match.

Speaking of good friends, I will be visited here on Cape Cod on Monday by Paul Alan Smith for a couple of days. Undoubtedly we will talk about you behind your back. We will have fun. He thinks the world of you, as do I.

Keep on keepin' on, good friend.

Much love,

Howard

September 15, 2009

Hi Pablo,

This letter will no doubt cover a bunch of issues that I hope <u>only you</u> will understand. Please bear with me.

Last week I received your card from Cabo San Lucas informing me that you planned to be with Howard from the 7th to the 9th. The day after receiving your card I received a wonderful powerful letter from Howard. He mentioned that he was expecting you on the 7th and would have big fun with you. He also informed me (for the first time) about his health, e.g. loss of hearing, poor vision, can't walk far, can't stand long, and just turned 87 and feels that he hasn't much time to go. Since Roz died, he has been philosophical, as she was, and as I am, about coming to the end, because the important thing is that we have lived a good life. He wrote many positive words about me, adding that when I leave this earth I will know I have contributed to the moral development of future generations. His words touched deep into the marrow of my bones. He and I have been and remain solid loving friends and lifelong friends. We met 25 plus years ago. He guided me through my political science course when he was teaching at Boston College. I could go on and on with listing the many many special favors he has done for me. <u>He brought you into my life</u>. I'm going to hang tough until I can't walk, talk, read, write, type, play some music, eat, shower, shave, and tease your sorry ass. I don't want anyone to pity me or my situation, be it about being in prison or having prostate cancer. I need to read more of your crazy-ass way of teasing me and at the same time inspiring me. I want to again remind you how much I appreciate you coming to this hell-hole to visit. I really enjoyed seeing and talking with you. I was hoping big time to meet you esp. before I leave this planet.

I had to "talk" to you today. Bringing you into my thoughts and prayers brings me inner peace and strength and courage. I pledge my life to you and Howard.

❤ Many many thanks and incessant love, peace and respect. ❤

Tiyo

P.S. Whenever it comes to pass that you receive the fucked-up news that I died don't you dare shed any salty tears or say, "Oh shit!!!" If you do I'll come back and haunt the hell out of you! Move forward and live a life of love.

November 6, 2009

Hi Pablo—

Enclosed are two articles re: PA judges and the negative shit that has and continues to take place at this hell-hole. Plus, there has not been any heat on the tier that I and other "lifers" are on. The weather today is 29°! Whew! It's been like this for three weeks. The guards gave us one extra wool blanket. Jack Frost doesn't give a shit about wool blankets. Plus, the first case of H1N1 flu has arrived. That particular guy now stays in a special cell in the hospital. The staff is hopeful no one else gets the flu.

More bad news: The guards informed me due to my age and illness I am no longer going to be cleaning the showers. They fear if I fall out or slip and fall or just die when I'm down there, they will be blamed. In short, I no longer have a job. My pay was $28.00 per month. That allowed me to purchase toilet articles etc. at the commissary. I don't smoke or eat much food. Who needs food and drink? Maybe "they" are hoping I'll just die soon. Fuck 'em! I plan to hang around a long time and haunt the hell out of 'em! ☺

Some positive news: I've been offered a position on the editorial board at SUNY Cortland. I accepted! ☺ As I learn more specific details re: the position I'll let you know.

I'm also fine-tuning my recent essay for Mecke's new book. I sent a 1st draft to you. Will have final draft sent to you. Which reminds me. I received your groovy "notice" re: PEN-USA 19th Annual Literacy Awards Festival. Glad you mentioned George Bernard Shaw, one of my favorites. He had it right when he said, "Silence is the most perfect expression of scorn." ☺ I love it!

I'm sittin' on the bunk in this cold-ass cage freezin' my narrow colored ass off, yet strong & happy enough to hope you're doing okay, workin' hard, and being healthy. Can't thank you enough for looking out for us older guys, Norman Lear, Howard Zinn and me. We love you! ☺

Tiyo

Monty Neill and Tiyo

November 19, 2009

Yo Pablo! ♥

Thank you super much for sending the bottle of wine to Danielle Kovacs. (Check enclosed letter.) I love you muchly! ☺

Brief news update. Mecke Nagel, Ph.D., Head of Dept. of Philosophy at SUNY Cortland, offered me a position on the editorial board. Crazy-ass me accepted. She plans to visit me soon and explain my duties etc. She has mentioned that I'll be ask to focus on and write about prisons, prisoners and the criminal justice system and also respond to questions from students. I'll keep you posted.

I've sent letters to Howard Zinn regarding the bullshit that took place at UMass. See next page. Howard sent an email of protest. I too sent a letter of protest. Still no heat for those of us on slow death row. It's been really fuckin' cold. The guards gave me two extra wool blankets and allow me to stay in the shower room for one hour. Yesterday another "lifer" died! That makes 16 deaths in the first 11 months of this year.

Now to the UMass situation.

Erika Arthur, who is in the master's degree program at UMass, was helping to bring Ray Luc Levasseur to campus to give a speech. They have come upon quite an ordeal. The UMass chancellor and Rob Cox (who by the way is head of the W. E. B. Du Bois Library) have come under intense fire for hosting Ray. Some police organizations and right-wingers and the governor Deval Patrick took issue with Erika and other students and staff for hosting of a "terrorist"! So the event was cancelled. However, Erika is not giving up and is trying to reorganize the event to bring up issues of academic freedom and freedom to dissent. Zinn wrote an email of protest in support of the event. So Erika and the students asked him if he will speak as well. They are not sure if he can make it. In any case, they are trying to take this opportunity to expand the conversation even further. It seems very important at this moment in history. Erika, Howard, Rob Cox, Danielle and others are in my special network. That fact is the impetus for my letter of protest. I'm not afraid of the fucked-up system.

Tiyo

11-19-09

YO   PABLO ♡

Thank you super much for sending
the bottle of WINE To Danielle Kovacs.
(check enclosed letter). I love you muchly! ☺

Brief news update. Mecke Nagel, Ph.D, Head of Dept. of
Philosophy at SUNY Cortland, offered me a position on the
Editorial Board. Crazy ass me accepted. She plans to visit me
soon and explain my duties etc. She has mentioned that I'll be
ask to focus on and write about prisons, prisoners and the criminal
justice system and also respond to questions from students. I'll
keep you posted.

I've sent letters to Howard Zinn regarding the
bullshit that took place at UMass. See next page,
Howard sent an email of protest. I too sent a letter
of protest.

Still no heat for those of us on slow death row
It's been really fuckin' cold. The guards
gave me two extra wool blankets and
allows me to stay in the shower room for
one hour. Yesterday another "lifer"
died! that makes 16 deaths in the
first 11 months of this
year.

②

Now to the UMass situation.

Erika Arthur who is in the Master's degree program at UMass was helping to bring Ray Luc Levasseur to campus to give a speech. They have come upon quite an ordeal. The UMass Chancellor and Rob Cox, (who by the way is head of the (W.E.B. Du Bois Library) have come under intense fire for hosting Ray. Some police organizations and right wingers and the governor Deval Patrick, took issues with Erika and other students and staff for hosting of a "Terrorist" so the event was cancelled. However, Erika is not giving up and is trying to reorganize the event to bring up issues of academic freedom and freedom to dissent. Zinn wrote an email of protest in support of the event. So Erika and the students asked him if he'll will speak as well. They are not sure if he can make it. In any case, they are trying to take this opportunity to expand the conversation even further. It seems very important at this moment in history. Erika, Howard, Rob Cox, Danielle and others are in my special network, that fact is the impetus for my letter of protest. I'm not afraid of the fucked up system.

Tyo

2010
"THE LOSS OF OUR FRIEND"

Jan. 16, ~~2010~~

Dear Tiya —

I love your essay "A Call For the Abolition of Prisons" in which you make your case so clearly, so persuasively. You understand the tactical problem of persuading people and your idea of Healing + Caring Centers is sensible + appealing to any thinking person.

In solidarity,
Howard

P.S. I'm so glad the essay will have permanent power in Wessel's book

1-28-10

Dear Paul

I learned about the death of Howard
at 5 A.M Today.

I hope to hear from you soon.

Liz

February 9, 2010

Hello Pablo!

Thank you very very much for the huge package of emails. The words written by your friends regarding the loss of our friend Howard were beautiful, touching and truthful. You somehow knew that I needed to know much more regarding when, where and how he died. I knew you were hurting as much as I was. You handled yourself very well. You took charge and held yourself and others together.

I did not do well. In fact I almost had a serious heart attack. My B/P went up to 224 and the doctor gave me Lisinopril and Catapres and ordered me to stay in bed for 24 hours. I am 77 years and 5 months old. I try not to let that stop me from moving forward with various projects. I have a bunch of medical problems. I will not bug you about my problems. Later during this week I will write to you and explain the things Howard and I discussed over the phones. We had a great time talking and laughing and teasing about you.

I assume by now you have received a copy of the proposal I wrote re: restarting the Coalition for the Abolition of Prisons (CAP). There is <u>no</u> <u>need</u> for you to become involved with the project. I plan to go it alone for as long as possible. I "gotta" keep trying.

I truly hope you are doing okay. <u>Please, please, please</u> take care of yourself. Include me in the huge group of people who care about you and who respect and love you very much. We need you more than ever before now that Howard has left us.

♥ Tiyo

Pablo !

FYI 3-10-10

It was a close call for me. I almost didn't make it. I'm getting
better with each new day. I can
still kick your sorry ass! ☺

I love you Big Time!

Tiyo

To: Superintendent Walsh

From: Tiyo, AY-2414, I-Block

Tiyo

On March 2nd, 2010, I became seriously ill. When I entered
the infirmary Dr. Bohinshi and his staff gave me their
immediate attention and began giving me various important
tests. Dr. Bohinshi decided my condition warranted being
moved to the Wilkes-Barre General Hospital. Upon arriving
there, Dr. Samir Akach and his staff provided me with out-
standing care, concern and treatment. The attention given
to me both here and at the Wilkes-Barre General Hospital was
awesome. I appreciate your kind gesture of allowing me to
receive phone calls from my friends and supporters during my
stay in the hospital. My counselor, Mr. Judge did a fine
job of coordinating the required paperwork and checking with
the Unit Manager, Mr. Josefowicz regarding approval of a
special visit with my son and his lady.

I want to make it abundantly clear that I profoundly
appreciate the special treatment bestowed upon me by all the
people involved with this matter. They richly deserve
admiration. My heart overflows with joyous gratitude.

cc: Dr. Bohinshi
     Dr. Samir Akach
     Mr. Josefowicz
     Mr. Judge
     Mr. Joe Ryan
     Quaker Meeting
     Friends and Supporters

July 19, 2010

Pablo!! ☺

My dearest ever-lovin' sorry-ass lifelong mofo FRIEND! ☺

I received and read your toe-tappin' wonderful, informative, interesting, creative five-page typed letter. I truly enjoyed reading your written catharsis. Your words flow nicely and make clear your thoughts and ideas. Your analogy "Israel has become a House Negro" is, in my view, profoundly correct! I have some thoughts to relay to you that support your ideas to successfully expose deficiencies in a society.

Before getting into all that I want to explain a few things. First off, the reason this letter is not typed is due to the pain and numbness in my fingers and hands. My arthritis mixed with diabetes renders difficult problems moving my fingers on the typewriter, keyboard and sax. You'll have to deal with my poor-ass printing I used one finger typing the letter to the Cremation Society. Also, your groovy long-ass letter reminded me how (years ago) you and I typed long-ass letters to each other. Your long letter has inspired me to return the favor. Soooooo read on, mofo, Read On! ☺

Allow me to lay a little historical background on you. Howard and I would often discuss the question can nonviolent resistance be a more powerful tool to achieve a Palestinian state than rockets and missiles? Many Palestinians define "nonviolence" to include stone-throwing. You wrote, "If one is ever going to successfully expose deficiencies in a society, theirs or someone else's, he must be humble and respectful. Consequently, he must have the ability to first criticize or withstand criticism of his own ways and habits and hypocrisies first." I totally agree. Allow me to explain why I agree with your statement. From Howard Zinn I learned that passion and commitment can be combined with openness and inclusiveness. He did so with warmth and wisdom that have inspired me ever since. It is a gift of inestimable value.

Many times I've asked myself, what does my life mean and what does the future hold? In my view, it's about committing yourself passionately to the choices you make. Yet we are both aware that life at times is messy and imperfect as are human beings. You are indeed blessed to be among the few human beings to realize how fucked up the thinking and social engineering via the power elite has brought, e.g. wars, destruction to the environment, politics and social chaos, etc. Check out for example the Declaration of Independence, which in my view is a masterpiece of rhetorical idealism that was followed by the U.S. Constitution, which is also a masterpiece of ambiguous practicality. The combination of rhetoric and ambiguity appeared in the Bill of Rights itself, in the 5th Amendment, e.g. 1857 Dred Scott decision (non-person to be returned to slavery). All thought up and written up by a group of power elite slave-holding white mofos. Most folks don't know much about history nor about critical analysis. The educational systems in the world are mostly fucked up. After meeting and learning from Howard Zinn, I was surprised that millions of people read his book, the People's History, and began thinking and organizing positive creative ways to fight the power. Still, there is no unique powerful people's revolution/organization that will give birth to a permanent solution to the present crisis, not just in the Middle East but worldwide. I totally agree with you that a new activism/revolution is needed. I would love to attend and hear you give a presentation of your ideas/words that you wrote in the letter. No one will listen to me, an old fucked-up sick prisoner whose time on this planet grows short. It's gonna take you and people like you to get the mofo job done. You have the gonads and tools needed to start the "proverbial ball" rolling on the right path. You have a humongous monumental prodigious task ahead. You will have to deal with all kinds of folk, e.g. some rabbis, both in Israel and elsewhere, have decreed that it may be permissible to take the life of any person in a position of power who takes part in dismantling a settlement or trades land for peace. A lot of Christians are as blind and narrow in their thinking/faith as Jews and Muslims. Traditionalists tend to be suspicious of the present and think the only way to go forward is to go back. Liberals tend to think that tradition is oppressive, so the future, however, will simply be a reiteration of the present. For me, I think our best future will be a creative remix of everything we are and have been. I gotta add a few words regarding the force of fear. Fear is always what's behind trying to preserve what one perceives as the truth in a coercive, threatening way. Check how FEAR was used by G. W. Bush regarding WMD to go to war in Iraq. The crime bill signed by Clinton, the new immigration bill in Arizona, etc. Members of both parties in Congress use the Fear Card as do local and state government officials. We need to create new workable and acceptable kinds of conversations on how to unify people around the globe in the pursuit of peace, reconciliation, and open-mindedness. While living around prisoners I learned among many other things, that I could not be their teacher until I was willing to be their student. By the way I love the new word you created, e.g. "systemicism". I also dig the way you use the words, "house negro". ☺ You know when, where, and how to use the right type words to get your point of view over and to jolt the mind to thinking and enjoying new important learning. Another important sentence that you wrote, "We simply are not disciplined to support one another and that contributes greatly to our consistent lack of progress at a time when we simply don't have much to piss away." Wow! I love it! For years and years I've been writing and speaking to prisoners and various so-called progressive organizations. That sentence is the <u>major impetus</u> why it's so fucking difficult to abolish prisons and the death penalty, wars, racism, pollution of the water, foods, air, inequal distribution of wealth, child labor, and a host of other negative laws and thinking. Talk about destructive behavior! Whew! By the way, why do you write and send me such powerful fuckin' letters? You know lots of powerful, rich people both nationally and internationally. Me, I'm just a 78-year-old fucked-up "colored" prisoner who happens to be dirt poor and lacks any kind of political clout. Very few people know I exist. Ha! Sooooooo it's <u>you</u> who must do all the shit work. I learned profound wisdom in Howard's work and his message. I listen and learn much from your work, messages and travels.

I gotta include my two-cent thoughts regarding Hollywood movies and TV power brokers. Here we have the means to really educate and reach people worldwide. The focus should be truth-telling regarding world history, e.g. Zinn's <u>People's History</u>, and promoting your ideas and the ideas of folks like you. These huge powerful machines are being wasted with dumbass programs that manipulate the minds of the general public, e.g. a large segment of prisoners are hooked on soap operas and cartoons and, of course, sports. Pool tickets are posted every week, esp. on basketball and football games. The thugs who can hardly read or write talk lots of shit about the point spread and the names and positions and other stats, yet cannot explain the reasons why they are being fucked over by the criminal justice systems. The powers that be learned how to control the majority of prisoners. Give "'em" dumb TV and movies, plus food 3 times a day and bullshit vocational/educational programs limited to 20–25 prisoners out of 2,218 prisoners. As you are aware poverty breeds prisoners. You are facing a huge difficult task. I truly feel hurt inside because I'm not "out there" to help you nor will I be around much longer to cheer you onward and upwards. I am super super happy that Howard introduced you to me and me to you. ☺ You guys have helped save my life and inspired me to work hard to educate white, black, brown and

Asian thugs for as long as I'm able, and to sometimes have a lot fun doing it. Look at how your long-ass lovely letter moved me to respond in kind.

Yes, I'm just as fucked up as you are, maybe even more so, yet we can deal with our craziness in a positive creative manner because of our ever-expanding incessant bond and friendship. It's a soulful true groove to be one of your many lifelong friends. The test of loving yourself is that you are able to love others more fully. When we are truly seeking, we uncover the best in all of us. Thank you for your beautiful and powerful letter.

Love you muchly!
Tiyo

November 2, 2010

My dear and most loving lifelong friend,

I am hurting deep within the marrow of my bones because I know you are hurting due to the passing away of your father.

I wish I were able to be "out there" and close by your side to give you some warm groovy hugs and to try to make you smile. I've been in a daze ever since receiving and reading the letter Jordanna sent me. Please know that I've been touching and talking to your pictures and praying for you and all your family members. The past month has been full of stress for me. Please hang in there my friend. I willing would give my life so that you would live. I will stay in closer touch with you.

I love you muchly!
Tiyo

Tiyo Attallah Salah-El
AY-2414
1000 Follies Road
Dallas, Pennsylvania 18612-0286

11-2-10

My dear and most loving life-long Friend,

I am hurting deep within the marrow of my bones because I know you are hurting due to the passing away of your Father. I wish I were able to be "out there" and close by your side to give you some warm groovy hugs and to try to make you smile. I've been in a daze ever since receiving and reading the letter Jordanna sent me. Please know that I've been touching and talking to your pictures and praying for you and all your family members. The past month has been full of stress for me. Please hang in there my friend. I willing would give my life so that you would live. I wish stay in closer touch with you.

Thinking of you!

TIYO

I love you muchly!
Tiyo

Long Live Peace, Justice, Love and Great Music.

Tiyo with his good friend and correspondent Monty Neill, who introduced Tiyo to Howard Zinn in 1982. November 16, 2009.

2011
"YO MOFO!"

Introduction

The handbook you are holding in your hands is a modern day educational tool written by a prisoner and edited by his friend, Lois Ahrens. The positive learning experiences by prisoners who have used the contents of this book have proven that there are creative and productive ways for prisoners to prepare for and pass the GED. To do this, you must study and study hard.

Many prisons in America house two, three, four thousand or more prisoners. As of 2008, 2.3 million men and women are incarcerated in the United States. The number continues to grow. Most prisons are limited in providing space and staff for educational and vocational services. Prisoners need proof they have a high school diploma or GED before they can participate in pre-release programs. Not having access to GED classes creates an obstacle which prevents prisoners from moving forward.

If you are a prisoner and in need of a GED in order to gain pre-release status or to be recommended for outside clearance, or a better paying job, make more phone calls, be allowed special visits or parole, we strongly suggest you take part in this opportunity.

This program allows you to study sometimes alone in the cell and also in groups of two, three or four. This program will give you self-empowerment. You control when, where and the number of hours and what subjects you focus on. In other words, YOU are in charge of your learning and education.

History of This Program

This program began during the year 2004. Four prisoners learned that I have a Bachelor's degree in African American History and a Master's degree in Political Science. They requested my help regarding their desire to attain a GED. Within two months, I put together a program that included social studies, science, mathematics, reading and writing. I based this course of study on GED materials that had previously been used in this prison.

I tutored the four prisoners for five months, spending about two to four hours per day, five days a week. When they felt confident in themselves and in control of their studies, they applied to the education department to take the yearly GED tests in the school. Their applications were accepted and they took the GED tests. They received high marks and were awarded a GED. News of their success brought more requests from prisoners to become involved in this program. Over time, I enlisted the help of some of the men who passed the GED tests to become tutors of other men. In this way, we were able to rapidly increase the number of men taking and passing the GED. Our success rate climbed and news of the program spread. In a four year period, more than 280 prisoners were tutored by other prisoners. 263 prisoners took their GED tests and 242 passed!

September 13, 2011

Yo Mofo!

I began writing to you on 9-11-11. Now it's 9-13-11, which by the way is my 79th birthday. I guess that shows as I grow old I take longer and longer to get things done. ☺ Some of the crazy things that have happened during the past 2–3 weeks I could not control, e.g. the horrific flooding in this area and areas close to this prison. Most of the guards that were on the 6 a.m.–2 p.m. shift could not leave because most of the 2 p.m.-10 p.m. guards could not make it to this prison due to the flooding of roads etc. The power went off causing a lockdown for app. two days.

The following week another lockdown including major cell and strip searches all day into the night. We were fed peanut butter & jelly, 2 slices of bread, 1 green apple and a small box of milk. I used some of the money you sent me to buy some soups, tea, honey, crackers, a small bag of Tang, and a bunch of toilet articles. I'll skip relaying news regarding drugs, fights, love affairs, etc.

I want to relay the news that during all the craziness that happened, you (yes, you) and your powerful proposal kept running around in my brain <u>every fuckin' day</u>! Cut to the chase----you are <u>on point</u> and you are telling the <u>truth</u> re: climate change and the urgent need for people to begin NOW to put your ideas into action **NOW**!! If people refuse to accept and put into action your plans to begin riding bikes and getting off their lazy asses and stop polluting the water, air, food, etc., this planet is **<u>DOOMED</u>**!!!! Time is running out! I'm going to try to help you as best I can, e.g. maybe write a tune that will catch on, or write a letter or letters to various editors, or ask everyone in my network to ask all the people in their networks to get on board or to contact you. I'll keep trying as long as I live to do what I can from this cage to help you. This project is no doubt my final mission on this earth. I willing and proudly give my life to you and <u>in memory of Howard Zinn</u>! I love you muchly! Hang in there! We will **win** this battle!

♥ Tiyo

2012
"I'M TAKING TIYO HOME WITH US!"

January 9, 2012

HAPPY NEW YEAR! ❤
Yo Mofo!

I wish you huge, triumphant, prosperous and happy success this New Year and the remaining years of your life.

This letter will focus on my health and an overview of what the doctor recommends. I am, to the best of my knowledge, the oldest prisoner here, e.g. I'll be 80 this coming Sept. 13th. On December 26, 2011, while in this cage reading the New York Times, I became ill and was taken to the hospital via a wheelchair. On 12-28-11, the doctor examined me, checked the EKG and B/P heart rate, etc. and ordered a bunch of pills for me to take.

I have arthritis in my lower back, hips and both legs. If I stand in one spot for 4–5 min my legs become numb with pain. Same with my hands. Add my heart problems to this situation and my age, small wonder I'm still living and rippin' you every chance I get. Anyway, the doctor suggested I buy a pair of sneakers, sweat pants, sweatshirt and go to the gym and get on the treadmill and slowly (very slowly) exercise my legs. He signed me up to report to the hospital from 12-29-11 until 1-13-12, for B/P and heart rate checks. He also suggested I locate two guys to walk with me to the gym and help me on and off the treadmill and to make sure I drink lots of water and do not fall down. After Jan. 13th, I'll send you the card the doctor gave me that will show the results of some of my B/P, heart rate, etc. I am not proud to be the oldest mofo here. However, I'm very pleased to still be alive. Yip-pee! ☺

I hope you are doing okay and are as fucked up in the head as ever.

❤ Tiyo

March 8, 2012

Yo Mofo!

Some good news, some strange news and some Fucked-Up News! First, the good news.

Huge huge hugs and super thanks for the New York Times and the book from the Museum of Modern Art!! WOW!! I showed it to the thugs and they turned into kids in a candy store. It's a first for all of them. Word is spreading about the book all around this prison. These mofos NEVER EVER seen such photos or even heard of the Museum of Modern Art. (Whew!) The book by Connie Rice is (for me) a page turner. From the beginning of her story, esp. meeting that young black kid who asked her, "What is you?" Also, the in-depth background of her mom, dad, sister, brothers, and grand and great-grands, and great-great-grands and others, her sitting next to the kid who smelled of urine due to problems with his kidneys. Also, the little white girl who was barred from jumping rope because she had a "nigger friend", viz. Connie. I don't want to get to carried away writing this to you, but I can relate to a lot of what Connie had to deal with growing up. It's almost a re-run of me growing up. I'm only halfway into the book. I'll let you know when I complete it. Again, thanks for both of the books.

Some fucked-up news!! (Yikes!) Last week I almost fell out in the chow hall. The guards rushed in and placed me in a wheelchair and took me to the prison hospital, where I stayed for a few days. The cause of the problem was due to a mistake by one of the medical staff giving me the wrong medication. It's good my body is still strong enough to recover from such mistakes. I received IVs and other stuff, and soon was back on my feet. I refuse, totally refuse, to die. Yippeeeeeee!

Finally—3 more staff members were escorted out of here. This place is full of looney staff members. Thugs continue to "somehow"???? enter this prison. It's become a fucking joke. The word is that the women were selling pussy not just to prisoners but also to some of the guards. It appears that there is a thin line between prisoners and some staff members. Not many people refuse pussy.

Please allow me to get super serious. I will soon explain a number of reasons why your friendship and support are very important to me. I want you to know the many things I've learned from you and how you saved me from killing myself. You entered my life at the time I was planning to say goodbye. I'm confident you are fully aware of the fact that my health is not good. In a strange yet happy way you inspire me to "keep moving on" in a positive and respectful manner and continue to help others as best I can. You are a special & talented human being. I'm writing a story about you and me. Stay tuned!

Love,
Tiyo

May 11, 2012

Dear Pablo—

Do you remember Joe Ryan? He was the superintendent of this prison. He was in charge when some of my Quaker friends escorted Howard into the prison to visit me. Ryan retired years ago but stayed in touch with me via the mails.

Yesterday, Joe and his wife Kate surprised me with a special visit; not in the visiting room but in the gym during the retiree breakfast. They remembered your name. I was allowed to escort them to the main gate where Joe told the guards,

"I'm taking Tiyo home with us!"

The guards just laughed and refused to let me go. Maybe next time Joe comes to visit me, the guards will let me go home with him. Such an event would make national news.

Hang in there!
Tiyo

SEPT. 9, 2012

DAVID

    AS YOU RECEIVE THIS LETTER, YOU MUST BE
WONDERING WHY NOW AND WHAT FOR, AFTER ALL
THESE YEARS? NOT IN THE HABIT OF CORRESPONDING
TO ANYONE THESE DAYS WITH MY ARTHRITIC HAND,
I NEVER THE LESS WANT TO EXPLAIN THE REASON.

    AFTER GRADUATION, MOST OF US WENT OUR
SEPARATE PATHS WITH LITTLE OR NO CONTACT WITH
EACH OTHER, WITH THE EXCEPTION OF SOME OF
THE GIRLS GETTING TOGETHER FOR LUNCH A COUPLE
OF TIMES EACH YEAR. THEY DECIDED, AFTER MANY
YEARS, THAT WE SHOULD HAVE A REUNION. SEVERAL
OF THEM TRIED TO TRACE EVERYONE'S LOCATION
AND WERE SUCCESSFUL, WITH THE EXCEPTION OF
MARY BOWMAN. OUR QUEST CULMINATED WITH OUR
FIRST REUNION IN 2000, FIFTY YEARS AFTER GRADUATION.

    IT WAS VOTED ON, THAT WE WOULD MEET EACH
FALL WITH AS MANY CLASSMATES ATTENDING AS THEY
COULD. THE GIRLS THAT WERE STILL MEETING FOR
LUNCH IN APRIL THOUGHT IT WOULD BE NICE IF THE
MEN WOULD NOW ATTEND THAT LUNCHEON WITH
WIVES AND FRIENDS ALSO. IT WAS DURING THIS
PERIOD OF TIME THAT WE WERE ALSO COGNIZANT
OF THE LIST OF THOSE WHO WERE DECEASED.

    DUE TO YOUR SITUATION, WHICH MOST OF US WERE
AWARE OF, WE SAW THAT YOUR NAME WAS ON THAT
LIST. THE YEARS PASSED BY AND I WAS

READING THE OBITUARY LISTINGS ONE DAY A COUPLE OF YEARS AGO ANT NOTICED THE PASSING OF YOUR SISTER. WITH WONDER IT LISTED AS A SURVIVING BROTHER, DAVID OF DALLAS. HOW COULD THIS BE I WONDERED. I SHOULD HAVE SATISFIED THAT WONDER SOONER THAN NOW, I KNOW. THIS LAST SEVERAL MONTHS I FIND MYSELF THINKING OF YOU WHILE AWAKE AT NIGHT, DURING PERIODS SOME DAYS AND DECIDED TO CONFIRM THAT YOU DO LIVE.

ABOUT THREE WEEKS AGO I WANTED TO GET AWAY FOR AWHILE AND DRIVE UP TO ROUTE SIX AND OVER TO WELLSBORO AND ON. I WAS CLOSE TO DALLAS AND DECIDED THEN TO LET YOU KNOW SOMEHOW YOU WERE BEING THOUGHT ABOUT BY SOMEONE. FOR DIRECTIONS, I STOPPED AT THE DALLAS POLICE DEPT, WHERE THE CHIEF OF POLICE WAS MOST HELPFUL IN USING HIS COMPUTER AND WAS ABLE TO VERIFY YOU ARE ALIVE AND NOW NAMED TIYO.

HE ADVISED ME A TRIP TO THE PRISON WOULD NOT ACCOMPLISH ANY ADDITIONAL INFO AS I ALREADY KNEW I WASN'T ON A VISITATION LIST. DAVEY, AS I KNEW YOU OR TIYO AS YOUR KNOWN NOW, I KNOW YOU NOW AS YOU WISH TO BE NAMED, WITH COMPLETE ACCEPTANCE.

I CALLED YOUR CHAPLAIN AND HE ALSO THOUGHT THIS TO BE THE BEST WAY TO COMMUNICATE MY FEELINGS TO YOU. YOU MIGHT LET ME KNOW IF YOU WOULD WANT TO HEAR FROM OTHERS IF THEY ARE WILLING.

I CAN TELL YOU I AM SO SORRY YOU ARE WHERE YOU ARE, AND I DON'T KNOW WHY, BUT I HOLD NO ILL WILL FOR YOU, AND ONLY WISH THINGS COULD HAVE BEEN DIFFERENT. I STILL HOLD YOU AS THE MOST POPULAR AND FUN LOVING PERSON OF OUR CLASS AND WISH YOU ONLY THE BEST YOU CAN MAKE IT IN YOUR SITUATION. I REALIZE THERE ISN'T MUCH ANYONE CAN DO TO MAKE A DIFFERENCE, BUT IF THERE IS LET ME KNOW.

REMEMBER, YOU ARE IN SOMEONE'S THOUGHTS. STAY HEALTHY, HELP OTHERS AND SURVIVE.

A FRIEND

Dick Brittingham

P.S. A LIST OF
CLASSMATES NOW
DECEASED.

VERNON BRITTINGHAM
CARROLL CLARK
WEBB CROSSON
JACQUELINE DRIESBACK
BARBARA HARLAN
JAMES MASSEY
MARY LEE RICHARDSON
PAUL RICKABAUGH
WILFRED ROBINSON
MARJORIE SLIDER
DAVID WALTON
SAMUEL WILSON
HELEN YOUNG

GUESS WHAT ?

COPY OF YOUR PICTURE
AT GRADUATION TO ME.
ON THE BACK IT READS—
ALWAYS A PAL,
JONES
1950

1950

Tiyo and Dick Brittingham's high school graduating class of 1950.

September 1, 2012

Yo Mofo!

Erika and I had a fine time together. We included you in our discussion of many topics. She is AMAZING! Smart as hell! Also down to earth and funny; sharp wit. I enjoy talking about you to our friends, viz. Monty Neill, Lois Ahrens, Mecke Nagel, and Marina Drummer, plus a "cast of thousands"!

Last night (Wed.), the second shift guard gave me 12 bricks of ice cream and 12 cupcakes. The 3rd shift guard gave me a large pizza. Both guards wished me a happy "fatty" birthday. I shared the items with the MOVE brothers and 3 of my ex-students, and 3 old guys who do not receive mail, visits or phone calls. I downed the rest of the stuff. All things considered I had a rather hip 80th birthday. I'll be the guest speaker at your sorry-ass 80th birthday party.

Hang tough my friend and stay positive and in touch.

Warm groovy hugs,
Tiyo

12 28-12

TO: Paul Alan Smith

FROM: Tiyo

This is Dick and Karlene Brittingham.
Dick located me after 50 years. They
visit me every month. I talk about
how you take excellent care of me. And
Howard Zinn introduced me to you.

Tiyo's friends Dick and Karlene Brittingham visit him at SCI Dallas in December

2013
"I'M STILL ALIVE"

May 10, 2013

Yo sorry-ass Mofo! Eek! ☺

Yes, it's me again, your lifelong friend who has a large, **very large front yard**!!!!
Yip-peeeee! (Do you want to see it?) Stop playing with yourself and read this
amazing letter. I have some *good* news to send your way.

First off, I am well, reading, writing, organizing, meeting some interesting folks, listening to jazz and classical music, receiving monthly visits with
my classmate Dick Brittingham and his wife, Karlene, letters, cards from Monty
Neill, Erika Arthur, Lois Ahrens, Marina Drummer, Mecke Nagel, Danielle
Kovacs, Vahram Elagöz, Justin Piché(see enclosed), and finally, a special visit
with the now-retired superintendent of this prison Joe Ryan and his wife, Kate.
I received dentures and have regained the weight I lost due to not eating solid
foods for app. 4 1/2 months. I am now ready to eat some "booty"! ☺

I noticed your name in The Progressive, that you will leave a legacy to the
magazine. Thank you muchly. Howard introduced me to The Progressive when
he and I first met and he provided me with subscriptions.

The seven thugs who are the best at completing the NY Times crossword
puzzles are planning to organize a contest, out in the main yard on July 4th.
They each will put 7 candy bars in a bag. The 1st, 2nd, & 3rd place winners will
divide up the 49 candy bars, plus be given 2 bags of chips. I will have copies
made of the puzzles during the month of June and present them to the guys on
the 4th of July. I'll keep you posted.

Finally, I hope you are doing well and that your new company is moving
along in a positive and productive manner. I will continue to "stay out of your
way" and not bug you with the dumb shit that goes on at this prison. I'll send
brief notes every now and then just to let you know I'm still alive. I'm not ever
going to stop fuckin' with you or die.

Take good care of yourself. Best wishes,
Tiyo

August 13, 2013

Yo Mofo!!

Our 4th of July New York Times Crossword Contest was a **huge** **huge** **freakin'** **success**!!!!! Thugs were standing 3 rows deep in the sun cheering for their favorite player. The guards <u>left</u> <u>us</u> <u>alone</u>!! Whew!! Some even stopped by to smile and say a few kind words. What was really surprising was the contests went on for four days for app. 1 hour each day. Many bystanders pitched in by adding candy, fruit, coffee, tea, hard-boiled eggs, chips, crackers, popcorn, etc. Two gay guys sang a song to the winners, which had everyone laughing and clapping! It was a funny and crazy-ass sight. They all want to continue to do the same during other holidays. You would have enjoyed it. I spoke about you and our special crazy-ass relationship/friendship, and that you supply us with the New York Times. I showed your sorry-ass pictures (just the good-looking ones!). Yikes! They all send their greetings and best wishes and thanks to you!!

We love your sorry ass! ☺ ♥
Tiyo

God bless you!!

November 2013

Yo Mofo!

Yes, it's me your one and only hardcore black lifelong friend! How "B" "U"?? I'm becoming more and more as bad as you are regarding staying in touch. Sorry about that. I make no excuses but there is a reason. Allow me to briefly explain.

I have been busy helping to organize the 2014 International Conference on Penal Abolition (ICOPA). People from Canada, France, England, Africa, Central/South America, Germany, Australia, the U.S.A. and other countries plan to attend. Academics, intellectuals and social justice activists of all shapes, sizes, and color, gay, straight, ex-prisoners, and others will be part of the conference during 2014/2015. I am on the steering committee. I'm writing a 2,000/3,000-word essay to be read by my friend Mecke Nagel, Ph.D. More about this later on, I have another positive project regarding music. Stay tuned!

My health is so so. My hands are shaking more and more with each new day and I'm moving around a bit slower, lot of pain in my body but not in my dick!! Eek! Yip-peeee!! ☺ Still able to read and write a lot. Can't type as fast as I once did. I don't eat much food, but I drink lots of water/milk, green tea with honey and have at least one wet dream per month. This place continues to go downhill; drugs, love affairs with female staff and prisoners, fights, racism, bad food, bad medical/dental care, no GED programs, nothing positive for prisoners to turn to and learn something to help them change their lifestyle. It's sad and tragic. It's a huge waste of billions of taxpayer money.

Okay---I gotta go!! Hope you and your company are doing well. I hope you are taking time to get laid at least once every two weeks. Relay my greetings to your cats. I'll do better staying in touch. Send me 4 black hos!!

I love you man!

Best wishes,
Tiyo

2014
"A RATHER STRANGE YET WONDERFUL EVENT"

February 10, 2014

Yo Mofo!

A rather strange yet wonderful event took place last Friday evening. At app. 9 p.m. I turned on my TV and lo and behold the story of Alice Walker was being featured. Within 10–15 min. guess who popped up on the screen? Yes, yes, yes, our lifelong friend, Howard Zinn!! He spoke about his time at Spelman College, meeting and talking with Alice Walker, his thoughts about her thinking, writing and books.

    Seeing, listening and hearing his voice, his thoughts and gazing at the pictures of him that I placed on the wall of this cell filled my heart with joy. When I later went to bed/sleep there was a huge happy smile on my face. I slept like a newborn baby!! ☺ I carry him in my heart and soul, and I do the same about you. You & Howard saved my life. I love and respect you guys very much. Hang in there!

Tiyo ❤

May 12, 2014

Yo Mofo, Mofo, Mofo!!

I've been working my narrow light-skin ass off writing my tribute to you, Zinn and a cast of millions who helped save my life and inspired me to never give up! When I first got busted I was a really dumb Negro. ☺ I am now a smartass, intelligent <u>colored</u> ☺ guy. Eek!

In spite of the lockdowns, fights, drug gangs, bad food, bad medical and dental care and racism, I stay above the fray. I stay many many hours alone in this cage <u>reading</u>, <u>reading</u>, <u>writing</u>, <u>writing</u>, <u>learning</u> and <u>learning</u>, and best of all I enjoy it! I still help some guys to attain a GED and I've been asked to organize another NY Times Crossword Contest out in the main yard during the 4th of July week. That I will do, plus it will be a good change of pace for me to take a slight break from writing the tribute. I plan to include pictures of each person mentioned in the narrative. I'll keep you updated and will send the final draft to you for comments, editing and so on and so on and so on!! ☺ Stay tuned and get a job!!!!

I love you man!!
Tiyo

October 10, 2014

Yo Mofo!! ☺

Brief note. Check enclosed letter. I'll keep you posted re: how the program turned out.

      Prison was <u>again</u> locked down!! Yikes! Lots of crazy stuff going on.

      I'm hangin' on by my finger and toenails! It's <u>cold</u> around here. No heat on the cellblocks. Bad food etc. You honkies sure know how to fuck over Negroes!! Yikes!

      Hope you are doing well and are crazy as ever. I continue working on my tribute to you, Zinn and others. Stay tuned!!

Love you muchly,

Tiyo

To: Rob Cox
Danielle Kovacs
Aaron Rubenstein
From: Tiyo Attallah Salah-El

Thank you for selecting part of my collection to be displayed and discussed during the special program. I am deeply grateful for your invaluable assistance and moral support.

I am also indebted to my lifelong friends, namely Monty Neill, Howard Zinn, Paul Alan Smith, Erika Arthur, Mecke Nagel, Marina Drummer, Dick and Karlene Brittingham and Lois Ahrens. They freely devoted their talents, visits, letters, cards, pictures and passion for justice, and stirred my spirit constantly. They guided me to reach beyond the boundaries of prison. I developed into a positive, productive political thinker and a much better human being. I am honored and privileged to know, respect and love these wonderful people.

To the people attending this event, I ask you to think about and discuss among yourselves the following questions:

- Why is it that the United States has the highest rate of incarceration of all developed nations?
- Why is a disproportionate number of the poor and people of color in prisons?
- What should be the perspective on punishment, retribution, restitution, life without parole, also known as Slow Death Row, the death penalty and prison abolition?

Thank you for attending this program. I wish you good health, long life and success with your present and future endeavors.

Sincerely,

Tiyo Attallah Salah-El

2015
"MY FRIEND PHIL AFRICA"

January 23, 2015

Hi Pablo—

Thank you very much for your words and card. Things here continue to be difficult to deal with, e.g. the passing of my friend Phil Africa, who by the way was only 63 years old and an intelligent, kind, caring and great teacher and friend. We were close and lived on this same cellblock for decades. His brother Delbert continues to live on this cellblock. An investigation has begun regarding what caused Phil to die. He did not smoke, drink jailhouse wine, nor engage in any nefarious activities. He was big and very strong. Enclosed is a picture of him drawn by one of my ex-students. We signed cards and wrote letters to his family and friends. I'll keep you posted about the situation.

There was a really bad incident that took place 3 days ago, e.g. a prisoner attacked a guard with a large combination lock wrapped in a cloth and knocked out one of the eyes of the guard. 10 to 15 guards came running to this cellblock and jumped on the prisoner and punched and kicked the prisoner who yelled to them to stop. Blood was on the floor and walls. It was really bad. The guards carried the prisoner to the hospital then to the Hole!!

This prison was built to house 1,000 prisoners. As of today there are 2,480 prisoners, who are mostly young, viz. in their early 20s, busted for using & selling drugs, 7th–9th grade education, dragged out of school, just barely living day by day, no mail nor visits, no job skills. Most when released from here are sent back within 2–3 years if not sooner. They don't seem to give a damn about living a better life other than becoming a gang member and involved with drugs. It's really sad and tragic!!

Sorry to send such fucked-up news to you. I'm not in a good mood. I stay mostly alone locked in this cage trying to educate myself via reading, writing and gazing at and talking to the pictures on two walls of you and Zinn and our friends. You guys help keep me alive.

Gotta go. I'll write you soon, e.g. a long letter of events, respect, hope and love. Thank you for putting up with me and for sending me the New York Times.

Love you muchly,

Tiyo

*Please excuse poor printing. My fingers & hands shake & hurt a lot.

This is my Friend Phil Africa

LOUGHNEY 2014

A drawing of Tiyo's late friend, fellow prisoner, and MOVE Organization member Phil Africa.

February 9, 2015

Hi Pablo—

I'm trying hard to steer a path through the pain of losing a friend. My courage and concentration have been cracked. I've experienced grief's power to bewilder. Yet I'm fully aware that life goes on unabated. I'm striving to muster the strength and courage to move forward and regain my balance and focus on completing my tribute to you and our friends. Writing to you and others somehow makes the unbearable bearable. I request your patience. I'll not ever give up!! I owe you big time!!!!

Hang in there with me. I love you ♥
Tiyo

August 10, 2015

Yo Honky Mofo!

Because you have been in some hellacious negotiations for new office space and moving the company and fixing up the place, plus spending big bucks, plus revamping the talent department, finding and getting rid of some folks, e.g. plus Asian, Indian, and heaps of honkys of all shapes and sizes, I thought the time is right to invite you to spend at least two weeks in this cell with me. It's a great place to kick back, relax and watch a bunch of dumbass out-of-control thugs destroy themselves. Last week two stabbings, plus one prisoner ran naked down the main hallway, plus three gays were busted giving <u>free</u> or <u>low</u>-<u>cost</u> blow jobs. All the "kookies" are not in a jar!!

Don't feel bad if you are a bit out of shape. I'm ten times more fucked up than you. Some days my whole body is in pain. Next month on Sept. 13th I'll be 83 years old. My mind continues to work well and my love of learning and reading and writing "keeps on keeping on"!! I wish you would gain approval from the prison to send me a bunch of chocolate cookies with marijuana in them like you did for Howard. Don't forget whenever I die please mix some of my ashes with some cookies and pass them to some of your workers! The best way to live a long life, in my view, is to stay busy with positive projects, and never give up!! I stay mostly alone in this cage. I enjoy my own company plus writing fucked-up letters to you.

I came across a brief bit of interesting education news that may have a positive effect for prisoners nationwide, e.g. Pell Grants to be restored for prisoners. The plan would allow potentially thousands of inmates to gain access to Pell Grants that would cover up to $5,775 a year in tuition, fees, books and other education-related expenses. Education Secretary Duncan and the attorney general are expected to announce the program. I'll keep you updated. I may be able to help the program.

I hope things are going well for your mom and that you can still hear your dad's voice yelling at you!! ☺ I can still hear Howard's voice giving me advice on ways to survive and ways to help people. I talk to you every day!! Yikes!! By the way, do you think Bill Cosby "banged" Bruce Jenner who is now known as Caitlyn?? ☺ What is "de" world coming to??

Enough of this out-of-control gibberish. You bring out the worst in me. I was a nice low-profile Negro until Howard introduced you to me and me to you. You are more fucked up than me. I don't know why I put up with your sorry ass. Maybe it's because you pay for my NY Times subscription. Money and pussy get things done!! ☺ Years ago I told you if you could cook I'd marry your sorry ass. Get a cookbook!! I'm coming to live with you!! Eek!! <u>I am in harmony with you</u>.

Warm hugs and lifelong love and respect,

♥ Tiyo

2016
"COMMUTATION"

Yo Smartass Honky Mofo!!

Some "breaking news" to send to you that could really fuck your <u>unholeeeee</u> mind!! I'm seriously thinking about applying for commutation!! By the way, this particular thought came to my mind because it's Black "Negro" History Month. In and during the coming weeks I'll explain reasons I may "give it a go"!!!! What do you think? Should I?? Please remember Howard told me "<u>never give up</u>"!! Whenever I pass on I want people to know that I gave it shot. I seek your advice. I'm checking out what will be needed, e.g. the forms, the questions, supporting, etc. I have accomplished major personal and academic goals and positive change in my life. The task ahead will be arduous and will demand meticulous in-depth give-and-take discussions between people who support me. Please let me learn your thoughts about this matter. I gotta go. I'm scheduled for a midnight blow job! Yikes!! ☺

Love & respect you muchly,
Tiyo

6-10-16

TO: Superintendent Mahally

FROM: Tiyo Attallah Salah
      AY-2414, I-Block

Yesterday, I was informed by the I-Block Unit Manager, Ms. Cicerchia and
Counselor, Ms. White, that I have until June 20th, to locate someone to cell
with. I had the Z-code for decades. I have not caused problems at this
prison. I have a positive rapport with guards and staff members.

This coming Sept. 13th, I will be 84 years old. Since being here I've been
escorted <u>3 times</u> to the Wilkes Barre General Hospital regarding my heart
condition. In addition, I am also diabetic. I'm aware that my time on this
earth is running out, but to be forced into a double cell situation at this
time will surely shorten what time I have left!

I have attained high academic and musical goals. And I've helped many
prisoners get a GED. I have a wonderful network of lifelong friends, some
who visit me every month. I am presently writing another book. Being
double-celled would be exceedingly difficult for me to deal with. I implore
your support and assistance with resolving this matter.

                                        Thank you.

                                        Tiyo

June 11, 2016

Hi Pablo,

Things here have become truly fucked up!! Check out enclosed copy of the letter I sent to Mahally. He did not create the new policy. The regional deputy secretary for the Department of Corrections, Harrisburg, PA, is the mofo who helped create this shit. His name is Michael Wenerowicz, and by the way he used to work at this prison!!!! Yikes!!

I have app. 8 or 9 days left to locate someone to cell with or decide to be placed in the fuckin' Hole and die there. Some prisoners have decided to go to the Hole. The only prisoners allowed to live in single cells are the homos, guys with huge serious mental problems and serious physically handicapped dudes. I've sent word of this situation to Monty Neill, Lois Ahrens, Erika Arthur and my classmate Dick Brittingham and his wife who visit me every month, and of course you!! No need for you to call here and talk to Mahally or other staff. Please allow me the freedom to decide my fate. No need to pity me in any way, shape or form. I'll find a way to complete my tribute to you and others esp. Howard Zinn. Even if I'm placed in the Hole I will at least be allowed to read the NY Times and write letters, etc. Whatever happens I'll deal with it as best I can. I'll let you know Mahally's response when I receive it. Stay tuned!

Your lifelong loving friend,
Tiyo

July 14, 2016

Helloo ☺ **honkey Mofo!!**

Thank you very much for your long-ass email re: my serious black-ass major problem, e.g. being doubled up in an 8' x 10' funky cell with a possible KKK redneck who farts a lot. <u>Yikes</u>! Thanks also for the groovy card and the news that you contacted the folks in Harrisburg, Penna, viz. Dept. of Corrections, re: my Z-code status. Reading your words brought me to tears and a massive two hour erection ☺ of joy!! I am honored and happy to inform you that all you did on my behalf **WORKED**!! <u>You sure in hell know how to get things done</u>!! If you were (a light skin colored female) and a "hot" virgin, I would marry your sorry ass.

Okay, allow me to relay the good news. Yesterday, at app. 2:30 p.m. I received official news that my Z-code single cell status <u>will remain in place</u> and <u>I will remain in this present cage on this cellblock</u>. <u>Yip-peee</u>! **Thank you**, **thank you**, **thank you**!!!! I will send word to Howard Zinn that you **saved my life**!!!! I plan to get some sleep and eat more food and regain the weight I lost during the past month. After that I will return to writing my "tribute" to you, Howard and others. <u>Please know I love and respect you muchly</u>!!

Warm hugs,
Tiyo

7-14-16

Helloo o honkey MoFo !!

Thank you very much for your long ass
email re my serious black ass major problem,
e.g. being doubled up in a 8' x 10' funky cell with
a possible KKK redneck who farts alot. Yikes!
Thanks also for the groovy card and ~~~~ the
news that you contacted the folks in Harrisburg
Penna, viz. Dept. of Corrections re my Z-code
status. Reading your words brought me to tears
and a massive two hour erection, ☺ of joy!!
I am honored and happy to inform you that
all ~~~~ you did in my behalf. WORKED !! You
sure in hell know how to get things done !! If you
were a ~~~~, (a light skin colored "female") ~~~~ and
a "hot" virgin, I would marry your sorry ass.

Okay, allow me to relay the good news. Yesterday,
at app. 2:30 pm I received offical news that my ~~~~
Z-code single cell status will remain in place and
I will remain in this present cage on this cellblock. Yippee!!
Thank you, Thank you, Thank You !!!! I will send
word to Howard Zinn, that you saved my life !!!!
I plan to get some sleep and eat more food and regain
the weight I lost during the past month. After that
I will return to writing my "tribute" to you, Howard
and others. Please know I love and respect you muchly !! Large hugs
                                                                                      Troy

July 14, 2016

To: Superintendent Mahally

I am pleased to inform you that yesterday I received notice
that my Z-code single cell status would remain in place.

I thank you and the staff who supported me in bringing about
a positive resolution to the problem I face. I have relayed
this good news to my lifelong friends.

                                    Sincerely,

                                    Tiyo

                                    AY-2414

CC: Paul Alan Smith
     (File)

October 16, 2016

Yo Mofo!!

Many moons have passed since my last letter to you. I apologizeeee for being a tardy dickhead. Please take under consideration that I is just another dumbass light-skin uneducated Negro! The redneck honkeees in charge of this prison, that is full of funky prisoners, continue to make things difficult to deal with. For example, lockdowns every week, strip and cell searches, poor food, gang fights about drugs and increased racissssm!! Due to my age and health issues some guards try to go easy on me and my books, papers, etc. and recently gave me an extra wool blanket to cover up with at nights. With all the problems I refuse to give up!!!! I spend time talking to and touching the pictures of you and Howard. That helps me to stay balanced and positive. I owe you big time!!! I shall try to be detailed, fastidious, upbeat and a bit cheerful with this letter and the enclosed materials. Please bear with my poor printing. My fingers and hands don't always work like they used to.

I received the large package of your letter and news about the passing of your mom. Your request that people not call you etc. was, in my view, the right call. I placed all the pictures of you and her in my photo albums. I've done the same with pictures Howard Zinn sent me. You guys are included in my thoughts every day!!

Check out enclosed letter from Caroline White. What an amazing surprise!! Go on Facebook to see my picture in color. Enclosed is letter from Cheryl Sturm, Esq. I've been in touch with her for app. 3–4 years. She sends me updates every month regarding federal and state decision. I would like to ask you to call her and discuss my chances of being granted commutation. You have lots of experience dealing with lawyers. She has an excellent record regarding poor people, esp. prisoners and others. She is tough and a fighter. Lois Ahrens, of The Real Cost of Prisons, called Cheryl regarding my chances etc. Lois left the decision up to me. I thought since I'm writing my tribute to you, Zinn and others, that if I die while in prison, I want people to know I gave commutation a shot. Cheryl is aware that you played an important role regarding keeping me single cell. I enjoy informing people about our unique, strong friendship and the many huge special favors you have and continue to bestow upon me.

I hope this letter and materials have a positive impact on your sorry ass. Years ago I sent word to you that if you could cook I'd marry you!!!!! (Yikes!!) If you don't begin locating and putting some black male and female slaves to work for your company I'll turn in my membership card in the KKK!!

I shall try to do better staying in touch with your lazy uneducated, race-baiting sorry ass. Hang in there with me!! Together we can change the world and smoke a ton of weed!! (Yip- peeee!!) I love and respect you muchly!!

♥ Tiyo

December 8, 2016

Yo Mofo ever-lovin' brother!!!! ☺

Enclosed is a copy of the letter from Dr. Kathleen Brown, who has offered to help me put together a strong well-written application for commutation. Lois Ahrens sent it to me. I'm sending copies to you and Monty Neill to check out and to learn how difficult the commutation process is.

It will take a lot of time, study and discussion between all of us, plus victory may not come my way. All I can promise is I'll try my best. This state is super hard on lifers. Look at the numbers, e.g. six lifers released during the past 22 years. Please don't get your hopes high. It could be that I only get one bite at the apple. Hang in there with me. My love and respect for you continues to grow.

♥ Tiyo

2017
"THE PROBLEM WITH MY EYES"

February 15, 2017

Yo Mofo!!!!

I apologizeeee for being tardy writing. I've been dealing with problems of my eyes. I've been to the outside hospital twice and scheduled to go back at least two more times. I can hardly see out of my right eye. My left eye is in bad shape. The doctor will operate on my right eye first and then when it heals will operate on my left eye. I asked our crew of friends to relay word to you. Stay tuned!! Am I still your only real live Negro friend!!

I love and respect you muchly!!

Tiyo

May 11, 2017

Yo Mo!!!!

I apologize for not writing to you like I used to do a long time ago. The problem with my eyes continues and is the reason for my poor large printing. I was told that I'm blind in my right eye and within 9 months to a year my left eye will not be working. I contacted a lawyer, viz. Agos Love who sent me some legal materials about the settlement his staff made with the PA Department of Corrections. I sent the copy to Lois Ahrens and asked her to relay copies to you and our friends. When I locate the new updated power-of- attorney materials and other related materials I will ask Lois to relay the materials to you and others. Please stay tuned!!!!

There is no heat on the cellblocks. 4 weeks ago heat was turned off. My left hip and leg are not working well. My body is slowly wearing out. (Yikes.) This coming Sept. 13th I'll be 85!!!! (Yikes.) I plan to hang around until I reach 100 years of age. Plus, I don't ever give up easily. Plus, I enjoy giving you a hard time. All I really need is a pound of medical weed and a big butt, big bust black ho!! Whenever my eyes get better I'll return to giving you pure hell. Stay tuned!!

I love and respect you muchly!!!!!
Tiyo

5-11-17

Yo MO !♡♡♡

I Apologize For Not Writing To
You like I used To do A long
Time Ago. The problem with my
Eyes continues and is The reason
For my poor large printing. I was
Told that I'm blind in my Right Eye
And within 9 months To A year my
left eye will Not be working. I
Contacted A lawyer, viz. Agus Love.
Who sent me some legal materials about
The settlement his staff made with
The PA Department of Correction. I
Sent The copy To Lois Ahrens And
Asked her To Relay copies To you And
our friends.

(OVER)

②

When I locate The New updated
Power of Attorney materials and other
Related materials I will ask Lois To
Relay The materials To you and others,
Please stay Tuned ?!!!

There is no heat on The cell block.
4 weeks ago heat was Turned off.
My left hip and leg are not working
Well. My body is slowly wearing
out. (yikes). This coming Sept. 13th I'll
be 85!!!!(yikes) I plan To hang around
until I reach 100 years of Age. Plus,
I don't ever give up easily.   Plus, I
Enjoy giving you A hard Time. Ah I
Really Need A pound of medical
weed and a big butt big bust black Hoe!!
Whenever my eyes get better I'll Return to
giving you pure hell. Stay Tuned!!
I love and Respect you muchly!!!!
Tyc

August 8, 2017

Yo Mo!!

I am very pleased to relay the good news that the operation on my right eye went well. At long last I can see again!!!! I'm looking at your pictures as I write this long overdue letter. <u>I've missed writing to you very very much</u>!! I want to thank you for all you have done and continue to do to help me <u>survive,</u> <u>thrive</u> and stay alive!!!! ☺ You spur me to think properly and interpret properly and to do so with vividness and vigor. You have given me positive reenforcement. You and Howard Zinn are my heroes and my champions and my lifelong loving friends.

Stay tuned!! I'll be in touch soon again.

Warm hugs, much love and respect,

Tiyo

8-8-17

Yo Mo!! ♡♡

I AM VERY PLEASED TO RELAY THE GOOD NEWS THAT THE OPERATION ON MY RIGHT EYE WENT WELL. AT LONG LAST I CAN SEE AGAIN!!! I'm looking AT YOUR PICTURES AS I WRITE THIS LONG OVER DUE LETTER. I'VE MISSED WRITING TO YOU VERY VERY MUCH. !! I WANT TO THANK YOU FOR ALL YOU HAVE DONE AND CONTINUE TO DO TO HELP ME SURVIVE, THRIVE AND STAY ALIVE!!!! ☺ YOU SPUR ME TO THINK PROPERLY AND INTERPRET PROPERLY AND TO DO SO WITH VIVIDNESS AND VIGOR. YOU HAVE GIVEN ME POSITIVE REINFORCEMENT. YOU AND HOWARD ZINN ARE MY HERO'S AND MY CHAMPIONS AND MY LIFELONG LOVING FRIENDS. STAY TUNED!! I'LL BE IN TOUCH SOON AGAIN.
  WARM HUGS, MUCH LOVE AND RESPECT.
      Tryo

November 4, 2017

Yo Mofo!!

Don't ask me why I continue to love and respect you so much! Maybe one day I'll find the answer to that question. I'll "keep on keeping on" trying!! Stay tuned!!

Soooo very sorry to be tardy writing to you. Please hang in with me. Lots of things going on. Check the following. The operations on both my eyes went well. My sight improves with each new day. Within the coming two weeks I'll receive new glasses. This past Wed. I had a nice positive meeting with my counselor and the unit manager regarding applying for commutation. They informed me that they and other high-ranking staff members will support me. They suggested I begin the process. I have a copy of the application. In the coming weeks I'll send a copy to you.

Now that my sight is getting better I started working on writing my "tribute" to you, Zinn, Monty Neill, Lois Ahrens, and others who have helped me survive, thrive, stay alive and become a better person. All you guys are very special people and are truly my lifelong loving friends. This past Sept. 13th was my 85th birthday and I'm feeling very good. No major health problems. I will keep you informed about both of my major projects, viz. commutation and my tribute. All I need is 10 pounds of excellent weed and 4 hos!! Please know that I will always love and respect you muchly!!!!

Tiyo

2018
"I LOVE YOU MUCHLY"

January 9, 2018

Yo Mofo!

Thank you muchly for your wonderful well-written letter and the photo of Hep
Cat, plus the copy of the notice you sent to folks regarding your recent speakers
soirees. Am I the only light-skin black guy to receive your notice???? I'll discuss
this matter with Howard. Stay tuned!!

     I want to express my thoughts about certain parts of your powerful letter.
I ask that you relay my greetings and best wishes to the mother and her two kids
who lived next to your mom, who fed your sorry ass and helped you during a
stressful time. Send warm hugs and thoughts to them via the airwaves. By the
way, thank you extra much for all you did, e.g. calling here re: getting the much-
needed operations on both my eyes. I owe you <u>huge</u> <u>lifelong</u> <u>love</u> <u>and</u> <u>respect</u>!!!!!
Howard and I will take you out to dinner and offer you 5 pounds of excellent
weed to smoke!! Yip-peeee!!

     I almost wet myself when I read in your letter that you saved all my let-
ters and you hired an experienced TV executive to put all the letters in chronological order!! Whew!! Check the following—I have done the same with all
your sorry-ass letters. I have tons of letters, cards, pictures, etc., magazines,
copies of The Progressive, and other reading materials, and of course Howard's writings, etc. Enclosed are some of my papers etc. that are housed in the
W. E. B. Du Bois Library at UMass. Later on I'll explain more about this matter.
I'm amazed that we both had the same idea without telling each other until
now. Stay tuned!!!! ☺

     Also included is a copy of the application for commutation. I sent word to
Monty Neill and Lois about my thoughts why I need your help. I am not able to
complete the application. The questions are difficult. I have worked many hours
and nights searching and drafting possible appropriate responses. I am over-
whelmed with fatigue and strain. I'm in need of your help. My options are limited. I think it best that I seek legal assistance. I ask that you contact Monty and
Lois and discuss my request for legal help. Please excuse poor printing. I'll do better next time. Give some nice warm loving hugs to Hep Cat.

Whatever you decide about my request, know in advance that I made a promise to Howard that I would always love and respect you until I die. You have helped me to survive, thrive and stay alive and to take care of you.

 I love your sorry ass!!

Tiyo

☺

February 12, 2018

Yo Mofo-er!! ☺

Thank you very much for your 12-30-17 letter and all of the wonderful groovy news, plus the beautiful pictures of your mom's dogs! I'm already deeply in love with those dogs!!!! WOW!! The gifts you continue to bestow upon me fill my heart with immeasurable joy. I shall relay this special news to Howard. ☺

You say that you are fixated on downsizing yet you have recently set up a new project, e.g. keeping the tons of old letters and cards, etc., and have hired a TV executive who is one of your long-time friends to organize the letters etc. in chronological order. Whew!!! Allow me to express some of my thoughts regarding your project. You have an effective vision that to me is clear, concise, easily understood, exciting and inspiring, challenging, stable but flexible, excellence centered, implementable and tangible. **Count me in**!!!! ☺ Please include words about Howard. I got your back!! Go for it!!

Please give Hep Cat my greetings and some groovy hugs and love from me. By the way, maybe you should keep some the kitchenware and tools you got from your mom and save them when I make commutation and move to be the only Negro living next to you. Yikes!! ☺ By the way, you take excellent care of me. You help me to stay positive and alive.

Warm loving hugs and incessant love and respect.

♥ Tiyo

April 29, 2018

Shalom, mi sorry-ass amigo!!!! ☺

Can't you read???? I made a request to you to send me a million dollars. I received the notice that you sent me $9.16!!!! Now I can fully understand the name <u>Pablo Bonehead</u>!! I used to think I was "<u>truly</u>" your anthropoid negroid colored lifelong loving friend. I'm on the brink of rethinking my thoughts about you. I plan to discuss this matter with Howard. Stay tuned!!

Enclosed are pictures of some of the bands I organized for various special events for outside guests and prisoners' talent shows. There is a picture of the outside band that asked me to join them for the program. By the way, I no longer play nor compose music. I sent my sax as a gift to Monty Neill and his wife to give to a young person who was in need of a sax. I now just listen to music, both jazz and classical music.

I received a very nice letter from Monty suggesting that I focus on writing a second draft of my application for commutation. He is an excellent teacher, supporter and lifelong friend. You and Monty are my true brothers. You guys saved me. I love and respect you guys <u>very</u> <u>very</u> <u>much</u>. I shall make a much better application for commutation. I give you my word and promise. I owe you guys and Howard Zinn big time. I'll not let y'all down in any way.

Give my greetings to your cat. Tell her (????) that I'm thinking about her and her health. By the way, please do not send me a million dollars!! I'd rather you send 50 pounds of weed!!!! Yip-peeee!! ☺

Warm loving hugs,
Tiyo

P.S. Please send copies of the pictures to Monty and Lois
Thank you!!

(Thanks for the $300.00. ☺ I love you muchly.)

May 6, 2018

Yo Mofo!! ☺

I returned the million dollar check Trump sent me to become his only favorer forever Negro prisoner. I do not know how he got my name and address, nor do I want to sleep with "Stormy"!!!! ☺

I received letters from Monty and Lois that focused on suggestions for improving my first draft of the application for commutation. I've been working on putting together a better 2nd draft, e.g. how I organized the GED program, teaching music classes, working in the band room, playing with some of the outside bands that played here. I also helped with the various sports programs, the support I received from the superintendents and staff, and esp. from you, Monty, Lois, Mecke, and a "cast of thousands", and the Trilling Toe-Tapping visits with you and Howard!!!! They also suggested I ask my friend and 1950 classmate Dick Brittingham to write a letter of support on my behalf. I sent a copy of my prison activities my counselor wrote (Monty stated he would send a copy to you).

There is still a lot I have to do. It will take time to complete the final draft and typed. By the way, my hands are starting to shake. Please forgive my poor handwriting. I think I'm in need of some medical weed!! Thank you muchly for the many wonderful special favors you continue to bestow upon me.

Warm loving hugs and respect,
Tiyo

5-6-18

Yo MoFo!! ☺

I RETURNED THE MILLION DOLLAR
CHECK TRUMP SENT ME TO become
his ONLY FAVORER FOREVER NEGRO PRISONER. I
do NOT KNOW how he got My NAME ANd Address,
NOR do I WANT To sleep with "Stormy"!!!☺

*****************ALL FOR AC C 180
0408   40
0204186128488905960613 18
TIYO ATTALLAH SALAH-EL
AY2414 SCF@DALLAS
1000 FOLLIES RD
WILKES BARRE PA 18612

I RECEIVED letters From MONTY And Lois That
Focused oN suggestions For improving my
First draft of The Application For commutation.
I've been WORKING oN putting Together A better 2nd
draft, e.g. how I organized The GED program, Teaching,
music classes, working iN The band room, playing with
some of The outside bands That played here, I Also
helped with The VARious sports programs, The support
I Received From The superintendents And staff, And
esp. From you, monty, Lois, Mecke, And A "cast of
Thousands", And The Trilling Toe-Taping visits with you And
Howard ♪♪♪♪. They also suggested I Ask My FRIEND And 1950
classmate Dick Brittingham To write A letter of support in my
behalf. I sent a copy of my prison activities my
conseulor wrote, (monty stated he would send A copy To
you).

There is still A lot I HAVE To do. It will TAKE Time
To complete The Final draft And Typed. By The way,
my hands And starting To shake. Please FORGive my poor
hand writting. I Think I'm iN Need of some medical weed!!
Thank you muchly For The many wonderful special
FAVORS you continue To bestow upon me
                    Warm loving hugs And Respect.
                              Tiyo

ELECTRONIC GRIEF

May 23, 2018, 3:22 p.m.

To: Monty Neill, Paul Alan Smith, Mecke Nagel, Erika Arthur

I received a letter from Tiyo today. These are things related to his commutation. He received a letter from Bobby Ryan saying he would write a letter. And he writes that last week the shift captain informed him that the high-ranking guards will support his application.

Tiyo asked me and so did Erika about who should get the letters. I am fine with having them sent to me. Tiyo wrote in his letter than he will try to finish by September 13th, his birthday.

Tiyo wrote that he is writing about the crime: when, where, who and his remorse. This is good. He is also writing about his health—or rather ill-health.

In a letter I received a few days ago, he wrote that he <u>does not want to live in Chester, PA</u>. He said there is a VA hospital in Coatesville and that is what he thinking. He wrote that he will ask Dick Brittingham for help since he too is a vet and an American Legion member.

I think that's it for now.

Lois Ahrens

May 26, 2018, 9:49 p.m.

Thanks for this update, Lois. And for keeping track of the letters. I spoke with Dick Brittingham on the phone yesterday and unfortunately he relayed the news that Tiyo is in ill-health. They had tried to visit him on Thursday and were unable to as Tiyo had gone to the dispensary (i.e. infirmary?). Dick and Karlene were unable to get more specifics and went back home. When they got home there was a letter Tiyo had written advising them that he was unwell and that they should put off their visit until further notice. The letter also avoided details but Tiyo did say the medical staff was doing what they could for him.

Wish I had more and better info but wanted to pass on the word. Please let us know if anyone hears anything from him.

Best,
Erika

May 30, 2018, 5:06 a.m.

I just got a call from Louise, Tiyo's counselor, that he is in the Dallas hospital. From what she said, shingles turned into sepsis. He is very weak. She visited him this morning. He asked her to call me and Erika. He told her "I am not afraid to die" and she replied that was not an immediate concern, but it could be.

The head of medical is Leah Martin. I will give her a call. Out soon for rest of day, so may not reach her till tomorrow. Tho I have a health proxy, not sure what that means so long as Tiyo can make decisions, which he can.

Erika then called me and said if I could not get through, she could try this afternoon. I will be around next few days so will stay in touch as best I can. No idea about weekend but will try to find out how to get info.

Monty

May 30, 2018, 8:21 a.m.

Yes, he's at Wilkes-Barre General where I was also able to sneak in once and see him, bearing spring flowers, which seemed like a true miracle. I am seriously considering getting in the car and heading that way now.

Thank you, Monty, for getting in touch with Leah Martin and keeping us posted.

Erika

May 30, 2018, 11:13 a.m.

So sorry to learn this, Monty, and thanks for sharing with us immediately. Last time, I snuck to his hospital (was it 10 years ago?) and the 2 guards allowed me to sit with him.

Sorry I can't do the same now.

With a heavy heart from Barcelona,

Mecke

May 31, 2018, 3:26 p.m.

Hi everyone.

I called Dallas, got the medical unit. The woman who answered said the computers are acting up and she cannot pull up any files. She added that she knew nothing bad has been reported, so probably status quo. So more tomorrow, and I have added Ramona Africa to this list so she can forward info to Tiyo's close friend Delbert.

Monty

June 1, 2018, 9:20 a.m.

I talked just now with Leah Martin. The report from yesterday (which I suspect means yesterday morning given the route the reports take) is that he is stable. She read off: vitals are stable; he has acute renal failure, no elevated temperature, on IV fluids and antibiotics and pain meds; still in IC unit.

I will not be able to get info over the weekend, tho my name is in the computer for them to contact if they feel necessary (not that they will, of course). On Mon morn I can get the Friday report, then later Mon can get the Mon report. I will keep at it.

Have a good weekend. I know he is in our thoughts.
Monty

June 1, 2018, 10:56 a.m.

Thanks Monty.

Just spoke to my friend who treats kidney disease. She said that people can recover from acute renal failure. She thought that maybe because of the shingles, Tiyo became dehydrated which caused a lot of stress on his kidneys and so renal failure. The shingles, she said, are a way for infection to enter the body which is why he probably ended up with an infection. Pain meds are for the shingles.

I was thinking about "compassionate release." A LONG SHOT for sure. The "compassionate release" law was changed but it doesn't seem for the better. This is from a 2017 article in Prison Legal News: "Otherwise, only the people with the most articulate, aggressive, and demanding family members have a chance," he stated. That appears to be the case; from 2010 to mid-2015, only nine Pennsylvania prisoners were granted compassionate release. The state currently has an estimated 5,370 lifers who are expected to die in prison, and many other prisoners will not outlive their sentences. Disgusting.

Lois

June 2, 2018, 5:45 p.m.

I had an idea to get a message to Tiyo. Instead of calling the hospital operator and asking for Tiyo/David Jones, I called and asked to speak to the nurses station in the ICU. At first she didn't want to transfer me but she finally did. I spoke to a nurse and he said Tiyo was not in the ICU. He said it was pretty empty up there and he would know if he was and he looked at the list of people just to double check and he isn't in the ICU. So, that's it for my idea. I guess we will have to wait until Monday for an update.

Lois

June 4, 2018, 11:28 a.m.

Hello all,

I just spoke with Kimberly Harris, one of the nursing supervisors at SCI-Dallas, and she let me now that Tiyo is back at the prison, in the infirmary there. He got back at 6 p.m. last night. He is stable and his vitals look good. They are doing more lab work and assessing what kind of care he needs now in regard to his kidneys. She said he is his usual self, talkative and energetic, though he needs to rest. Mx. Harris was very forthcoming with information and encouraged me to call whenever I wanted updates. The computer was acting up again and I said that seems to happen a lot and she explained that they are using the electronic health records system, which is constantly being loaded with more data, and she suspects their computer infrastructure just can't handle it. It sounds infuriating, really; she expressed deep frustration.

I asked her about how they make decisions about if/when they transfer people to other facilities based on their health needs and she said that it's based on what kinds of specialized care Tiyo might need. Like if it turns out he needs dialysis, they can't do that there, so they would have to find somewhere else for him to go, which depends on availability. I asked her if they could notify his family/friends about these decisions and she said they don't usually, but that if there are multiple options and one of them is closer to people who visit him, then they would want to choose that one (I am not naïve to the fact that everyone who makes these decisions may not think the way she does). So it seems like we should keep checking in regularly right now so if these kinds of decisions are being made that maybe they could be informed by the fact that Dick & Karlene visit him regularly and wouldn't be able to if he were moved to western PA, for instance. Okay, I think that's all I have for now.

Erika

June 5, 2018, 9:51 a.m.

I just talked with Leah Martin. She says Tiyo is in a good deal of discomfort. Doc is prescribing pain meds. Said she saw him or another staffer reported to her that he was not his usual self this morning. She remains concerned. However, she said docs conclude his kidney function is OK enough to not need dialysis. I said I'd check in after a few days. Perhaps someone else can call tomorrow so we can have a daily flow of info.

I assume Delbert is seeing Tiyo, but if you would like to stay on this list, Ramona, it is certainly fine with me.

Monty

Jun 5, 2018, 9:59 a.m.

Ramona can say if Delbert can visit Tiyo. I have no idea what the rules are and even if it is allowed if they follow them at Dallas.

I am sorry to say I have very very little faith in what the prison doctor concludes about Tiyo needing dialysis or anything else. Why pain meds? Still from the shingles? I can call if no one else will do it. I don't think I'm the best person.

Lois

June 6, 2018, 8:00 a.m.

Just spoke with Leah Martin. She seems to think the pain meds are helping Tiyo's pain (primarily caused by the shingles)—he slept through the night and is stable. He is considerably deteriorated, she said, weak, in bed, not up and around. I asked if he is able to get visitors from within the prison (Del) and she said he's probably not up for visitors, but they do have a hospice program where other inmates are sitting bedside with patients. As for visitors from outside, she gave me the extension of Dep. George Miller (a relatively new deputy), who would be in charge of allowing this (which is usually not allowed except for deathbed visits, but who knows). In regard to dialysis, she seemed to think they wouldn't have discharged him from WBG if he needed it, but they're still waiting on bloodwork that would show this for sure. If he needed it, the facility she named that he would go to is Laurel Highlands, which is indeed in western PA.

I asked her to tell him we are thinking of him and calling to check in.

If y'all have immediate ideas for research that needs to happen on the compassionate release front, please let me know. I will try to look around in the next few days. And keep calling the prison.

Thanks,
Erika

Jun 7, 2018, 11:14 a.m.

Dear all,

I just got a call from Joyce Wilson, nursing supervisor, who said she called me to see about a visit. Will be real hard for me to pull off from Boston. She would set up the visit with his counselor, get security clearance.

Clearly this is dire.

Erika, I think you talked about a visit, so if you can...

I don't have Dick and Karlene's number. Can someone contact them?

Anyone who can visit should call Joyce Wilson, daytime nursing supervisor, or Kimberly Harris, night nursing supervisor. I am terribly sad to be writing this.

Monty

June 7, 2018, 11:30 a.m.

Just spoke with Leah Martin and left a message for Dick and Karlene. I'm going to try to get down there.

Best,
Erika

Jun 7, 2018, 12:05 p.m.

I have been on the phone with the prison. Tiyo is not conscious and Leah Martin said they think he may not make it until morning. Erika, please let Dick and Karlene know. If they can visit, great. Leah is leaving for rest of day. She said it might be best to talk with Deputy Super Richard Keller; and if a clerk or someone picks up, to say this is about a deathbed visit. Keller told Leah who told me that they would allow someone in into the evening, but details have to be worked out.

Monty

June 7, 2018, 2:23 p.m.

Erika just called me. She is on her way to Dallas, driving from Maine. She has
talked with Keller about getting in, but likely not to arrive till it is too late tonight.
Either tonight or tomorrow morn she hopes to hold his hand. Tiyo is in their hospice, being attended to. She asked Keller if Delbert was seeing him, Keller did not
know.

Monty

June 7, 2018, 2:59 p.m.

I have a certificate which you probably do too, from the Cremation Society of PA. It says, "Paid in Full. September 24, 2000." I also have a copy of maybe the card you have that says "in the event of my death call 1-800-720-8221." Account # 19355. Dated August 22, 1996.

I am not sure who the right person is...have not heard the "counselor's" name before. What about any of these people?

Kimberly? Leah Martin? Joyce?

They are all nurses, I expect I'll reach one of them in morning. Mostly I just want them to know that he wants to be cremated and what IF ANYTHING they have on file.

Yes.

I have to leave right now, but tomorrow morning can start making calls if you don't want to do this Monty. I could also call Keller.

Lois

June 8, 2018, 5:43 p.m.

Dear friends,

I got word just before 5 a.m. that our steadfast friend Tiyo had passed on around 4:30 this morning.

I'm sad to say I did not make it down here to Dallas until too late last night to see him. I do have a copy of the cremation documents, which I will bring to the prison when their admin staff comes on at 8.

They had next of kin down as Bev Williams, but I gave them your number, Monty. Maybe you've heard from them already. I'll give you a call soon as well. I'll call Dick and Karlene now as well.

My heart is heavy at the loss of such a bright shining spirit that has been caged for so long, but I'm at peace with the thought that Tiyo is free. I sing in a hospice choir and I've been singing one of my favorite songs in our repertoire for Tiyo. The line especially for him is: "Let the love I've shared speak for me. When I come to the end of this road, let me lay down my heavy load, let the love I've shared speak for me."

All my best, and deep gratitude for you all,
Erika

APPENDIX: VISION OF THE FUTURE

An excerpt from Autobiography of Tiyo Attallah Salah-El *(2006)*

We go where our dreams carry us. I have a vision and strongly believe that unless major cultural and policy changes are made not only in regard to the prison-industrial complex and criminal justice system but also the reconstruction of the social, economic, and political policies for the benefit of the majority of people of all races, genders, sexual preferences, and workers of all kinds, that there will be a new and nasty twist to Keynes's caustic observation that "in the long run, we're all dead"! In my view the United States is headed toward catastrophic tragedy.

Wars, racism, corporate greed, pollution of the food, water and air; economic inequality, joblessness, the homeless, poor health care, production and sales of biological, chemical and nuclear weapons, the abuse of women and children are just some of the exploitation of the people and natural resources by the sinister family of capitalism. Prisons are just one of the many immoral noxious pillars of capitalism/imperialism.

Slavery and prisons go together hand in glove. They protect the ruling elite and are also used to reinforce the power and influence of the state. They provide a large number of jobs to lower-middle- and middle-class people living in rural and economically depressed areas. The ruling power elite are willing to spend billions in order to be protected from the lower classes and to continue to expropriate the natural and human resources in the world.

From the 1990s to this present time, there has been a desperate plight of blacks, Hispanics and poor whites trying to free themselves from the suffocating confinement of social imprisonment. Prisoners face seemingly insurmountable difficulties in efforts to obtain some breaking and healing space for themselves. The similarity in the situation of prisoners and that of minorities in the larger society is too striking to be written off as merely metaphorical.

Convicted criminals is the one category to which the Thirteenth Amendment's prohibition of involuntary servitude explicitly did not apply. Exploitation of prisoners' slave labor in the form of chain gangs and the convict-lease system continued after chattel slavery had ended, and survives today in the form of lucrative prison industries, which return substantial profits to state and federal treasuries because of their exemption from minimum-wage laws.

Already, the idea of restoring the prison chain gang is spreading. Once the states can provide these slave laborers to labor contractors to lease to private industry, fortunes stand to be made. Then, by denying money to education, the states will assure that their citizens remain ignorant of the history and abuses of prison labor.

From 1870 until the early 1900s, Louisiana had a convict-lease system. Samuel L. James's initial contract ran from 1870 to 1893, when it was extended another ten years. James obtained the contract through bribes. His crony legislators and officials created and protected his contract. For a modest payment to the state, James was entitled to complete authority to lease out convicts used as slave labor, and had rights to the facilities of Louisiana prisons. James died in 1894, a multimillionaire. Overworked, underfed convicts with little or no health care were dying at a rate of 20 percent by 1892. Disease, exposure and maltreatment were the leading causes of death. Life expectancy averaged six years. During the last decade of the system 840 prisoners died, 216 in 1896 alone, as brutality reached record levels.

For those who can't guess, a glance at any of the photographs of these nineteenth-century chain gangs shows that they were overwhelmingly composed of recently "freed" black men. If conservatism, "lock 'em up," "three strikes and you're out" and the call to build more prisons are best, perhaps there should be a return to the stake and torture chamber too. This is not as farfetched as it may sound, as elections not only in the southern states but also across America are turning into contests to determine which candidate can display the least regard for human decency—e.g., George W. Bush refusing to stop the execution of Karla Faye Tucker.

Screened from public visibility and immune from effective accountability to other branches of the government, prisons commit predictable abuses. Today there is almost nothing the prison administration cannot do, and does not do, to prisoners, including keeping them beyond the expiration dates of their sentences (via parole procedures declaring them dangerous or mentally ill). They can and do transfer prisoners far from their families; limit and restrict their visitors; censor what they read and what they may write; decide what medicine or other medical care they will or will not receive, what education they may or may not have, whether they will be totally locked up for days, weeks, months, sometimes for years, or enjoy limited physical freedom. Prisoners' personal property may be misplaced and destroyed; incoming and outgoing letters are sometimes not delivered, and in the extreme prisoners may be physically brutalized. Parole boards may deny or grant parole according to information that is unavailable to prisoners on the basis of criteria which, if they exist at all, are secret. On the grounds that parole is a privilege, not a right, these decisions are ordinarily not reviewable by the courts.

Prison administrators understand the vulnerability and powerlessness of prisoners, parolees, and their families. Some prison officials can and do act with total, arbitrary authority to avoid any action, whether legislative or judicial, or from the community or attorneys, which asserts a prisoner's rights or desires against the desires of the prison system. To add insult to injury, taxpayers' money is spent to pay the attorney general to oppose any attempts in court to change these conditions. Prison has two distinct faces; one for the public, which it presents through skilled public-relations personnel and a budget provided by taxpayers for that purpose alone; the other, to prisoners. Most of the family members of prisoners are taxpayers. I find that interesting, informative and stupid.

There is, no doubt, a certain paradoxical quality to the suggestion that a law enforcement agency should itself be a lawless operation with total disregard for and in frequent violation of the law. This seeming paradox will not, however, be unfamiliar to blacks and other minorities who have been well-educated as victims in the abuses of the law, evasions of the law, and violations of the law on the part of law-enforcement agencies.

Victimization of black people at the hands of law enforcement is nothing new in the United States. As slaves, they had the legal status of chattel or real estate and were totally unprotected by criminal law, though masters' property rights in their chattel were fully protected. Free blacks hardly fared much better. They were tried in separate courts, and could be enslaved as punishment for criminal offenses, as well as for nonpayment of fines or taxes. Slave patrols were empowered to punish freed blacks without trial. After the Civil War, emancipated slaves were doubly victimized by a repressive and discriminatory system of law enforcement, and by the widespread extrajudicial use of lynch law.

For the last three hundred years, law and lawlessness have gone hand in hand in contributing to the oppression of persons of color. The law itself has often been openly discriminatory and repressive, but repression has never been confined to the law. While many of the legal disabilities created by openly discriminatory legislation have been repealed or struck down by the courts, illegal acts of repression and discrimination, as well as legal but covert forms of these activities, continue unabated. Veiled from public consciousness by secrecy and insulated from other pressures, prisons have not even had to change appearances.

Opposition politics and freedom of the press, of speech, etc. have not been eliminated so much as they have been bypassed. The elite's command of vast wealth and its control of major universities and news media, as well as its access to almost unlimited resources of government, enable its ideas and programs to dominate the public forum almost free from strong challenge. Only when repression becomes so visible that all the nations see it, does much of the population receive even an inkling of what prisoners or radicals or black people and other minorities face every day. Take, for example, the beating of Rodney King, the Attica riots, the dragging and death of a black man in Texas, the Civil Rights Movement, Watts riots, and Waco.

The genius of the criminal justice system has been the extent to which it has accommodated itself to the heterogeneity of the American population. It might be very difficult to sustain lawlessness in prisons or in the criminal justice system if all the public were exposed it. But this never happens. Most Americans are never processed by the police, courts and prisons. With few exceptions, this unenviable experience is reserved for minorities with little money, for cultural deviants, and those with threatening ideas. The reason is not that these groups are the most criminal in society; the explanation lies in the systematic biases and discriminatory institutional practices which characterize the enforcement of the law as well as its legislation. The American justice system is riddled with racial and ethnic bias. The deeper more elusive problem underlying the crises in the justice system is the persistence of racism among Americans and in their institutions. They cloaked their current manifestation of racism in the law.

Which would better remedy institutional racism: to change laws or to change attitudes? In my view, it is easier to change a law than to change a mind. Getting people to acknowledge they need to change their attitudes has always been the hardest part of the job. In order to be sensitive to race, to be sensitive to diversity issues, everybody has to be involved. Changing the institutions requires a complex and multilevel approach. Even the most well-meant laws can become unjustifiably punitive for minorities. Establishing justice that is truly blind may be less about the right numbers than who has the right attitude.

In the context of existing law enforcement practices, the prison system helps to sustain the myth that certain groups of people (for example, blacks, the Spanish speaking, Native Americans, poor whites) are inferior, defective, dangerous, not to be trusted; it discourages challenges to the existing political and economic order by reminding members of those groups that the violence of the state can and will be unleashed against them if they get out of line. Through the systematic nonenforcement of laws against corporate and governmental crime it not only helps to sustain the existing political and economic order but allows that order to clothe itself with a false mystique of lawlessness. Much of the lawlessness in prison and the criminal justice system has been directed at those who are suspected of involvement in the efforts to either save their own lives or to bring about radical and revolutionary change in the system.

Lawlessness, racism and exploitation serve very real functions in the defense of imperialist, oligopoly capitalism. Racial prejudice may have been promoted for the crassest economic motives, but it can hardly be denied that many believed in the tenets of racism. Hatred can in turn lead to fear, which will move the state to react violently. It is equally plausible that what seems like "overreaction" by the state can be interpreted as a perception on the part of authorities that their exploitative practices and mystifying ideology are extremely vulnerable to coherent organized opposition, which must therefore be suppressed at all costs. Opposition must therefore be co-opted and absorbed, or else crushed. Its survival would be too threatening. The ruling elite fear revolution. They are keenly aware the prisons are the potential seedbeds for revolution.

In spite of the enormous power and formidable inertia of the prison-industrial complex and the criminal justice system, there is a chance of achieving a future more in accord with the vision of freedom on which past generations of Americans were nourished. This chance is sufficient to support a rational, radical and revolutionary hope of reversing the trends that have led to the present day of overkill and public malaise.

The will to resist and to try for something better is an important component in the struggle for peace and freedom. Of course, to desire something strongly enough to fight for it does not guarantee success. But it changes the odds. The renewal of the abolitionist movement is not impossible. It is already coming together in various places in America and abroad. The dream may seem to some improbable, but it will become finally impossible only when the last dreamer gives up trying to make it come true. Henry David Thoreau stated, "Go confidently in the direction of your dreams! Live the life you've imagined." I choose to go in the direction of my dreams, and help bring revolutionary change in the world. To do so from a prison cell is rather unique and, personally, soul satisfying.

Embarking upon the road to revolution I first had to change myself. No one could do that but me. It was a combination of reading, writing, music, studying the history of various cultures, learning from my past mistakes, becoming a better listener and receiving the loving support from my family, friends and supporters that stimulated my imagination and inspired me to sharpen my skills and talents and gain the courage to take on the powerful penal system. During my journey I gained a sense of independence and personal dignity and discovered the power within myself.

Writing about my life, ideas and plans has been a labor of love. There were times when I had to deal with and resolve major setbacks—for example, having to ask my family and friends not to visit me because I refused to go through the degrading process of being strip searched in the visiting room; having difficulties reaching my sister Bette by phone during the time of her illness; having to file formal grievances against certain prison officials and dealing with and choosing to ignore negative remarks directed at me from some prisoners, guards and staff members. Does this mean that every prison warden and administration is malevolent or every guard mean and brutal? That every prisoner is denied medical care, or every prisoner placed in the "Hole" is falsely accused? Such is not the case. There are some good men and women working in prisons who are attempting to help prisoners overcome various causes that may have led to their incarceration. I have met such good people at the Dallas prison, namely Superintendent Joe Ryan, Captain Charles Coleman and Officer Sonny Womelsdorf.

Superintendent Ryan, who is now retired, encouraged me to pursue undergraduate and graduate degrees and provided access to professors from various area colleges and universities to send books and visit me in the visiting room. He also allowed me to play and record music with an outside jazz group that was later played by the local FM radio station. Although he retired some years ago, we stay in touch via mail. Captain Coleman and Officer Womelsdorf, both now retired, would also cheer me on by asking how I was doing with my studies, and providing time and space for me to study. They would read the results of my test papers and congratulate me on doing good work. They would also tease me a lot about being a hardcore dedicated Eagles football fan. During the times when things were not going well for me, they would take time to come by the cell and talk about ways to resolve certain situations. These men met with and talked to my sister Bette, whom they found to be a wonderful lady and my champion.

I indeed have been and continue to be blessed. I have accomplished some goals, remain in good health, able to play and write music, lift weights, read books, write lots of letters and send cards to my sister Bette and my many wonderful friends and supporters. I also take time to relax by feeding the birds, gazing at the moon and stars, dancing with and laughing at myself. I have managed to thrive and survive in the face of some of the most pernicious pressures imaginable. I know a lot about the pain that is the huge pillar of prison. I've paid some huge dues. My voice (words) comes from someone who's passed through the eye of a storm and came out shaken up a bit but standing tall, still willing to help right some wrongs, bring some hope, inspiration and justice into the lives of many people. Mostly I continue to give and receive love. I find it pure joy and an honor to give and receive love.

Arrangements are in place for my ashes to be spread by my close friends Monty and Shelley Neill, who upon learning of my death will gather together with some of their friends and listen to the music of John Coltrane, Miles Davis, and other jazz musicians and jazz singers, and eat a lot of good healthy food, drink lots of beer, wine, whiskey, scotch, laugh and dance and talk about some of the crazy yet happy times and things that took place in my life. No tears are to be shed for me. Long live love, close friends and beautiful music.

Peace and much love to all you guys who helped me thrive and survive!

To: Pablo

Tiyo

A drawing of Tiyo.

ACKNOWLEDGMENTS

Tiyo had a core posse, each of whom are worthy of having a national holiday in their honor. Their integrity, character and righteousness are humbling. They are: Lois Ahrens, Erika Arthur, Mecke Nagel and Monte Neil. Similarly, Caroline White, Rob Cox (may he rest in peace) and their colleagues at SCUA have been first rate, impeccably digitizing Tiyo's papers at the W.E.B. Du Bois Library.

A warm embrace to Dick and Karlene Brittingham, who were so kind and generous to Tiyo.

Shelagh Ratner, Beth Miller, Robyn Rosenfeld, Carrie Dolce and Lee Rosenbaum all helped get this project up and running.

Myla Kabat-Zinn has been supportive from moment one. Her approval for us to read Howard's letters provide a rare treat.

In a nutshell, this project would never, ever have been completed without my cousin John Kenney.

Thanks to my very close friend Bonnie Garvin, I met Michael Smith, who in turn got this book to the publisher at O/R Books, Mr. Colin Robinson. Nothing would exist without their initial support. Colin and his colleagues Teddy Ostrow, Marcus Hijkoop Emma Ingrisani, and Acacia Handel have been incredibly cool and patient. Antara Ghosh designed a spectacular book cover!

To the "Blurbers" Connie, Harry, Pam, Dick, Paul, Dave, Nomi, Michael, Robbie, Mr. Fish: A million thanks for permitting me to ruthlessly exploit your names; I am forever grateful.

An incredible audio version of this book was made thanks to the following super talented friends: Adam Arkin, Jerry Levine. Michelle Dunker, Wendy Shapero, Jack Daniel, Lance Guest and Danna Hyams. They not only contributed, but CRUSHED it!

A low, deep bow to Mr. Mike Africa, Jr. The fact that Tiyo's VERY FIRST LET-TER mentions Mike's "two brothers of the Move Organization" isn't lost on me. The generational connection between the three of them and Mike is one of the high points of my entire experience with Tiyo. To have their lineage connected, metaphysically/spiritually, still gives me goose bumps.

Lastly, I want to thank the truly extraordinary director/actor/entrepreneur Carl Weathers. Carl was beyond a generous partner on the audio version. Hearing Carl read Tiyo's words was a reward of such magnitude, I dare not diminish it with my rudimentary adjectives. Carl brought Tiyo back to life. It remains surreal, and hands down the highpoint of the project. What's more, Tiyo would have been over the moon to learn that Carl did this.

www.ingramcontent.com/pod-product-compliance
Lightning Source LLC
Jackson TN
JSHW011947131224
75386JS00042B/1600